COPENHAGEN

TRAVEL GUIDE 2024

Explore History, Culture, Hidden Gems, Cuisine and Local Secrets in the Heart of Scandinavia – Packed with Detailed Maps & Travel Resources

BY

MICHAEL VIANNEY

Copyright © 2024 Michael Vianney. All rights reserved. The entirety of this material, encompassing text, visuals, and other multimedia elements, is the intellectual property of Michael Vianney and is safeguarded by copyright legislation and global agreements. No segment of this content may be replicated, shared, or transmitted in any form or via any medium without explicit written authorization from Michael Vianney. Unauthorized utilization, replication, or dispersal of this content may result in legal repercussions, encompassing civil and criminal penalties. For queries regarding permissions or additional information, kindly contact the author via the provided contact details in the publication or on the author's official page.

TABLE OF CONTENTS

Copyright... 1
My Experience in Copenhagen... 5
Key Features and Benefits of this Guide... 7

Chapter 1. Introduction to Copenhagen... 12
1.1 History and Overview.. 12
1.2 Geography, Climate and Best Time to Visit... 14
1.3 Local Customs and Etiquette... 16

Chapter 2. Accommodation Options... 20
2.1 Hotels in Central Copenhagen... 21
2.2 Budget-Friendly Hostels and Guesthouses... 26
2.3 Boutique Hotels and Design Stays... 29
2.4 Apartment Rentals and Airbnb Options.. 31
2.5 Unique Accommodations: Houseboats and Eco-Friendly Stays......... 33

Chapter 3. Transportation in Copenhagen.. 35
3.1 Public Transport: Metro, Bus, and Train.. 35
3.2 Biking Culture and Bike Rentals... 37
3.3 Taxi Services and Ride-Sharing Apps... 39
3.4 Ferries and Water Taxis... 42
3.5 Car Rentals and Driving Tips.. 44

Chapter 4. Top Attractions and Cultural Heritage............................. 48
4.1 Tivoli Gardens and Amusement Park.. 50
4.2 Nyhavn Harbor and Colorful Houses.. 52
4.3 The Little Mermaid Statue... 54
4.4 Rosenborg Castle and Royal Residences... 57

4.5 National Museum and Danish Design Museum..................59

4.6 Hidden Gems: Off-the-Beaten-Path Discoveries............. 61

4.7 Cultural Events and Festivals...................................63

4.8 Outdoor Activities and Adventures.............................65

Chapter 5 Practical Information and Travel Resources.............68

5.1 Maps and Navigation... 68

5.2 Essential Packing List... 69

5.3 Visa Requirements and Entry Procedures.................... 70

5.4 Safety Tips and Emergency Contacts........................73

5.5 Currency Exchange and Banking Services................... 76

5.6 Language, Communication and Useful Phrases..............78

5.7 Shopping and Souvenirs....................................... 80

5.8 Health, Wellness Centers and Safety Tips...................83

5.9 Useful Websites, Mobile Apps and Online Resources........88

5.10 Visitor Centers and Tourist Assistance......................90

5.11 Recommended Tour Operators and Guided Tours........... 95

Chapter 6. Culinary Delights... 98

6.1 Traditional Danish Cuisine: Smørrebrød, Frikadeller........98

6.2 New Nordic Cuisine and Michelin-Starred Restaurants.......102

6.3 Street Food Markets: Torvehallerne and Paper Island........104

6.4 Coffee Culture and Danish Pastries........................... 106

6.5 Food Tours and Cooking Classes................................109

Chapter 7. Day Trips and Excursions................................. 115

7.1 Frederiksborg Castle and Kronborg Castle...................115

7.2 Roskilde: Viking Ship Museum and Cathedral...............117

7.3 Louisiana Museum of Modern Art...............................120

7.4 Malmö, Sweden: Öresund Bridge and Old Town............. 122

3

7.5 Hillerød: Frederiksborg Castle and Baroque Gardens..................... 124

Chapter 8. Entertainment and Nightlife... 128
8.1 Cafés and Bars in Nørrebro and Vesterbro.......................................128
8.2 Live Music Venues and Jazz Clubs..130
8.3 Beer Bars and Craft Breweries..131
8.4 Nightclubs and Dance Halls..134
8.4 Nightclubs and Dance Halls..137

Travel Journal...140

MY EXPERIENCE IN COPENHAGEN

In the heart of Scandinavia lies a city that captivates the soul and leaves an indelible mark on all who wander its streets. Copenhagen, the vibrant Danish capital which has woven its magic around my heart like no other place. My journey into the soul of Copenhagen began with a sense of eager anticipation, fueled by the countless stories I had heard and the enticing images I had seen. But nothing could prepare me for the overwhelming beauty and warmth that greeted me as I stepped foot in this enchanting city.

Wandering through the streets of Copenhagen is like stepping into a fairy tale. The colorful facades of Nyhavn, with their iconic wooden ships bobbing gently in the harbor, paint a picture of whimsy and romance that is hard to resist. I found myself lingering by the waterfront, savoring the sight of old sailors' pubs and vibrant cafes bustling with life. As I meandered through the narrow lanes of the Latin Quarter, I felt as though I had been transported back in time. The medieval architecture, adorned with intricate details and adorned with ivy, evoked a sense of wonder and reverence for the past.

From the majestic halls of the National Museum to the avant-garde exhibits of the Louisiana Museum of Modern Art, I found myself enthralled by the depth and diversity of Danish culture. But perhaps what struck me most about Copenhagen was its palpable sense of hygge, a Danish concept that embodies coziness, contentment, and the simple joys of life. Whether sipping hot cocoa in a quaint cafe or strolling through the serene beauty of the Tivoli Gardens, I couldn't help but feel a profound sense of peace and happiness wash over me. Of course, no visit to Copenhagen would be complete without indulging in its world-renowned culinary scene. From delectable Danish pastries to mouthwatering smørrebrød, the city offers a feast for the senses that is sure to delight even the most discerning foodies. I found myself eagerly exploring the bustling food markets and hidden gem eateries, each bite a revelation of flavor and tradition. But beyond its sights and flavors, Copenhagen is a city with a soul. It is a place where innovation and sustainability intersect, where bicycles outnumber cars and green spaces abound. As I pedaled through the city streets, I couldn't help but admire the Danish commitment to environmental stewardship and social progress.

My time in Copenhagen was nothing short of transformative. It was a journey of discovery and delight, a testament to the enduring magic of travel and the power of human connection. As I bid farewell to this captivating city, I knew that a piece of it would forever reside in my heart, beckoning me to return again and again.

KEY FEATURES AND BENEFITS OF THIS GUIDE

Welcome to the Copenhagen Comprehensive Guide, your ultimate companion to exploring one of Europe's most vibrant and captivating cities. Copenhagen effortlessly blends rich history with modern sophistication, offering a plethora of experiences for every type of traveler. Whether you're drawn to its charming cobblestone streets, innovative culinary scene, or world-renowned design culture, Copenhagen promises to enchant and inspire you at every turn. Let's embark on a journey through this dynamic city, uncovering its key features and myriad benefits along the way.

Maps and Navigation
Navigating Copenhagen is a breeze, thanks to its efficient public transportation system and well-connected network of bike lanes. The city's compact size makes it easy to explore on foot, but for longer distances, you can hop on a bus, train, or metro. Pick up a Copenhagen Card for unlimited travel on public transport and free admission to many attractions. Don't forget to download helpful navigation apps like Google Maps or Citymapper to effortlessly find your way around the city.

Accommodation Options
From chic boutique hotels to cozy guesthouses and budget-friendly hostels, Copenhagen offers a diverse range of accommodation options to suit every preference and budget. Stay in the heart of the action in districts like Indre By (Inner City) or Vesterbro, or opt for a quieter retreat in neighborhoods like Østerbro or Frederiksberg. Consider unique

accommodations such as houseboats or eco-friendly hotels for a truly memorable stay.

Transportation

Getting around Copenhagen is a breeze, thanks to its extensive public transportation network comprising buses, trains, and metros. The city is also renowned for its bike-friendly infrastructure, making cycling a popular and eco-friendly mode of transport. Rent a bike from one of the many rental shops scattered across the city and explore Copenhagen like a local. For longer journeys, consider taking advantage of Denmark's efficient rail system, which connects Copenhagen to other major cities and attractions.

Top Attractions

Copenhagen is brimming with iconic landmarks and attractions that showcase its rich history and vibrant culture. Marvel at the grandeur of the Christiansborg Palace, home to the Danish Parliament, or stroll along the picturesque Nyhavn harbor lined with colorful 17th-century townhouses. Visit the world-famous Tivoli Gardens, an enchanting amusement park dating back to 1843, or explore the cutting-edge architecture of the Copenhagen Opera House. Don't miss the opportunity to visit the Little Mermaid statue, inspired by Hans Christian Andersen's beloved fairy tale, which has become a symbol of the city.

Practical Information and Travel Resources

Before you embark on your Copenhagen adventure, it's essential to familiarize yourself with some practical information and travel resources to ensure a smooth and enjoyable trip. Denmark's official currency is the Danish Krone (DKK), and most establishments accept major credit cards. English is commonly used and comprehended, facilitating communication for visitors from around the world. Stay connected with free Wi-Fi available in many public areas, including parks, cafes, and museums. For emergencies, dial 112 for police, fire, or medical assistance.

Culinary Delights

Copenhagen has earned a reputation as a culinary hotspot, with its innovative chefs and thriving food scene drawing visitors from around the globe. Indulge your taste buds with traditional Danish dishes like smørrebrød (open-faced sandwiches) or frikadeller (meatballs), or sample contemporary Nordic cuisine at Michelin-starred restaurants like Noma or Geranium. Explore the city's vibrant food markets, such as Torvehallerne or Paper Island, where you can savor a variety of local specialties and international flavors.

Culture and Heritage

Immerse yourself in Copenhagen's rich cultural heritage by exploring its world-class museums, galleries, and historic landmarks. Discover the treasures of the National Museum, which chronicles Denmark's history from prehistoric times to the present day, or admire masterpieces by Danish and international artists at the SMK - National Gallery of Denmark. Delve into the world of design at the Danish Design Museum, or explore the vibrant street art scene in neighborhoods like Nørrebro and Vesterbro.

Outdoor Activities and Adventures

Embrace Copenhagen's outdoor lifestyle by partaking in a variety of outdoor activities and adventures. Take a leisurely stroll along the picturesque canals of Christianshavn, or enjoy a picnic in the lush greenery of Frederiksberg Gardens. Explore the city's waterfront areas by kayaking or stand-up paddleboarding, or venture further afield to nearby nature reserves like Dyrehaven or Amager Fælled for hiking and wildlife spotting.

Shopping

Copenhagen is a shopper's paradise, offering everything from high-end fashion boutiques to eclectic vintage stores and bustling markets. Explore the trendy boutiques and designer shops of Strøget, one of Europe's longest pedestrian streets, or hunt for unique souvenirs and handicrafts at the weekly flea markets in neighborhoods like Nørrebro and Vesterbro. Don't miss the opportunity to indulge in Danish design at iconic stores like Illums Bolighus or Hay House.

Day Trips and Excursions

While Copenhagen has more than enough to keep you entertained, it's also the perfect base for exploring the surrounding region's many attractions and natural wonders. Embark on a scenic day trip to the historic city of Roskilde, home to a UNESCO-listed cathedral and Viking Ship Museum, or venture north to the picturesque coastal town of Helsingør, where you can visit the legendary Kronborg Castle, immortalized as Elsinore in Shakespeare's Hamlet.

Entertainment and Nightlife

As the sun sets, Copenhagen comes alive with a vibrant nightlife scene that caters to all tastes and preferences. Enjoy live music and craft cocktails at trendy bars and jazz clubs in districts like Vesterbro and Nørrebro, or dance the night away at one of the city's many nightclubs and music venues. Catch a performance at the Royal Danish Opera House or enjoy a night of laughter at one of Copenhagen's comedy clubs. Whatever your nighttime pursuit, Copenhagen offers endless opportunities for entertainment and excitement.

This comprehensive guide serves as your indispensable companion to unlocking the secrets of this dynamic and culturally rich city. From its historic landmarks and world-class museums to its innovative culinary scene and vibrant nightlife, Copenhagen offers a wealth of experiences waiting to be discovered.

CHAPTER 1
INTRODUCTION TO COPENHAGEN

1.1 History and Overview

Copenhagen's story dates back over a thousand years, tracing its origins to a humble fishing village founded by the Vikings in the 10th century. Over the centuries, it grew into a bustling trading hub, its strategic location at the crossroads of the Baltic and North Seas making it a coveted prize for rival powers.

In the 15th century, Copenhagen emerged as the capital of Denmark, cementing its status as a center of power and influence in the region. The city flourished under the reign of King Christian IV, who left an indelible mark on its skyline with architectural marvels such as the Round Tower and Rosenborg Castle. But Copenhagen's history is not without its share of challenges and upheavals. In the 18th century, the city was devastated by fires and bombardments, leading to extensive rebuilding efforts that would shape its urban landscape for centuries to come.

In the 19th century, Copenhagen underwent a period of rapid industrialization and urban expansion, fueled by the rise of manufacturing and trade. The city's population swelled, and neighborhoods such as Vesterbro and Nørrebro emerged as vibrant centers of commerce and culture.

Today, Copenhagen stands as a testament to the resilience and innovation of its people, blending a rich tapestry of history with modern sophistication. Visitors are drawn to its eclectic mix of old and new, where medieval castles share space with cutting-edge design studios and sustainable urban developments.

As you wander through Copenhagen's streets, you'll encounter iconic landmarks such as the majestic Christiansborg Palace, home to the Danish Parliament, and the striking Marble Church, whose elegant dome dominates the skyline. But the city's charm lies not only in its grand monuments but also in its hidden alleys and cozy squares, where the spirit of hygge permeates every corner. From the canals of Nyhavn to the bustling markets of Torvehallerne, Copenhagen offers a wealth of experiences waiting to be discovered. Whether you're exploring the exhibits at the National Museum or sampling Nordic cuisine at a local bistro, you'll find yourself immersed in the vibrant energy and cultural richness of this captivating city.

But perhaps Copenhagen's greatest allure lies in its people – friendly, welcoming, and proud of their heritage. As you navigate the city's streets, you'll encounter a sense of community and warmth that is truly infectious, inviting you to become part of the fabric of Copenhagen life.

1.2 Geography, Climate and Best Time to Visit

Copenhagen's geographical layout is characterized by a blend of urban landscapes, waterways, and green spaces. The city is situated on the eastern coast of Zealand, Denmark's largest island, and occupies both sides of the strait of Øresund, which connects the Baltic Sea to the North Sea. The historic city center, known as Indre By, is located on the eastern coast, while newer neighborhoods sprawl across the surrounding areas.

Climate

Copenhagen experiences a temperate maritime climate, characterized by mild summers, cool winters, and moderate rainfall throughout the year. Understanding the seasonal variations in weather is crucial for planning an enjoyable visit to the city.

Spring (March - May): Spring heralds the awakening of nature in Copenhagen, with temperatures gradually rising and daylight hours increasing. The city is adorned with blooming flowers and lush greenery, creating a picturesque backdrop for exploration. Average temperatures range from 5°C to 15°C (41°F to 59°F), making it an ideal time for outdoor activities such as cycling along the waterfront or strolling through the city's parks and gardens.

Summer (June - August): Summer is undoubtedly the peak tourist season in Copenhagen, characterized by long days, abundant sunshine, and bustling streets. Average temperatures hover between 15°C to 25°C (59°F to 77°F), making it perfect for exploring outdoor attractions such as Tivoli Gardens, Nyhavn Harbor, and the iconic Little Mermaid statue. However, it's worth noting that summer also brings crowds and higher accommodation prices, so booking in advance is advisable.

Autumn (September - November): As autumn descends upon Copenhagen, the city is bathed in hues of red, orange, and gold as the leaves change color. Temperatures begin to cool, ranging from 8°C to 15°C (46°F to 59°F), and rainfall becomes more frequent. Despite the occasional showers, autumn is a delightful time to visit Copenhagen, offering fewer crowds and a more relaxed atmosphere. Visitors can enjoy cultural events, cozy cafes, and leisurely walks along the waterfront.

Winter (December - February): Winter transforms Copenhagen into a magical wonderland, with festive decorations adorning the streets and a cozy atmosphere prevailing throughout the city. Average temperatures range from -1°C to 4°C (30°F to 39°F), and while snowfall is not uncommon, it rarely accumulates significantly. Winter activities abound, from ice skating in Kongens Nytorv to exploring Christmas markets and indulging in Danish pastries and hot cocoa.

Best Times to Visit

The best time to visit Copenhagen largely depends on personal preferences and interests. For those seeking pleasant weather and vibrant outdoor activities, summer is the ideal season, albeit the busiest. Spring and autumn offer a balance of favorable weather, fewer crowds, and opportunities to witness the city's natural beauty and cultural events. Winter appeals to visitors enchanted by the city's festive ambiance, with the added charm of fewer tourists and the possibility of experiencing a traditional Danish Christmas.

Copenhagen's unique blend of geography, climate, and cultural attractions makes it a captivating destination year-round. By understanding the nuances of its geography and climate, visitors can make the most of their time in this enchanting Scandinavian capital.

1.3 Local Customs and Etiquette

Intriguingly, what sets Copenhagen apart isn't just its stunning architecture or scenic vistas; it's the intricate of local customs and etiquette that infuse every aspect of daily life. From the joy of cycling through its streets to the warmth of its kaffebarer and the culinary delights of smørrebrød, each tradition offers a glimpse into the heart and soul of this enchanting city.

Kaffebarer: Where Coffee Meets Community

Step into one of Copenhagen's cozy cafes, known as "kaffebarer," and you'll discover more than just a place to grab a cup of coffee. These establishments serve as communal hubs where locals gather to socialize, work, and unwind. Immerse yourself in Danish coffee culture as you soak in the warmth and camaraderie, experiencing firsthand the concept of "hygge" – a feeling of coziness, contentment, and togetherness that defines the city's cafe scene.

Smørrebrød Delights: Exploring Danish Culinary Traditions

Indulge your taste buds in the Danish tradition of "smørrebrød" – open-faced sandwiches bursting with flavor and creativity. From pickled herring to smoked salmon, each bite offers a delicious journey through Danish cuisine. Pair your smørrebrød with a glass of aquavit, Denmark's beloved spirit, for an authentic dining experience that captures the essence of Copenhagen's culinary heritage.

Hyggekrog: Embracing Cozy Retreats

In the heart of Copenhagen, discover the art of "hyggekrog" – cozy nooks that invite you to unwind and recharge amidst the city's hustle and bustle. Whether it's a window seat bathed in natural light or a snug alcove adorned with plush cushions, these intimate retreats offer a sanctuary from the demands of daily life. Embrace the Danish concept of hygge as you create your own personal haven, where comfort and tranquility reign supreme.

Jantelov: Embracing Humility and Community

Experience the spirit of "jantelov," a cultural mindset that emphasizes humility and egalitarianism, shaping the social fabric of Copenhagen. As you interact with locals, embrace the values of jantelov – listen more than you speak, celebrate others' successes, and cultivate a sense of solidarity within the community. In doing so, you'll gain a deeper appreciation for

Copenhagen's rich cultural tapestry and the warmth of its welcoming inhabitants.

Copenhagen's customs and etiquette offer a captivating journey through the heart and soul of this enchanting city. From its vibrant cycling culture to the cozy camaraderie of kaffebarer and the culinary delights of smørrebrød, each experience invites you to immerse yourself fully in Danish life. So, come and discover the magic of Copenhagen for yourself – a city where tradition meets innovation, and every corner is infused with the spirit of hygge.

CHAPTER 2
ACCOMMODATION OPTIONS

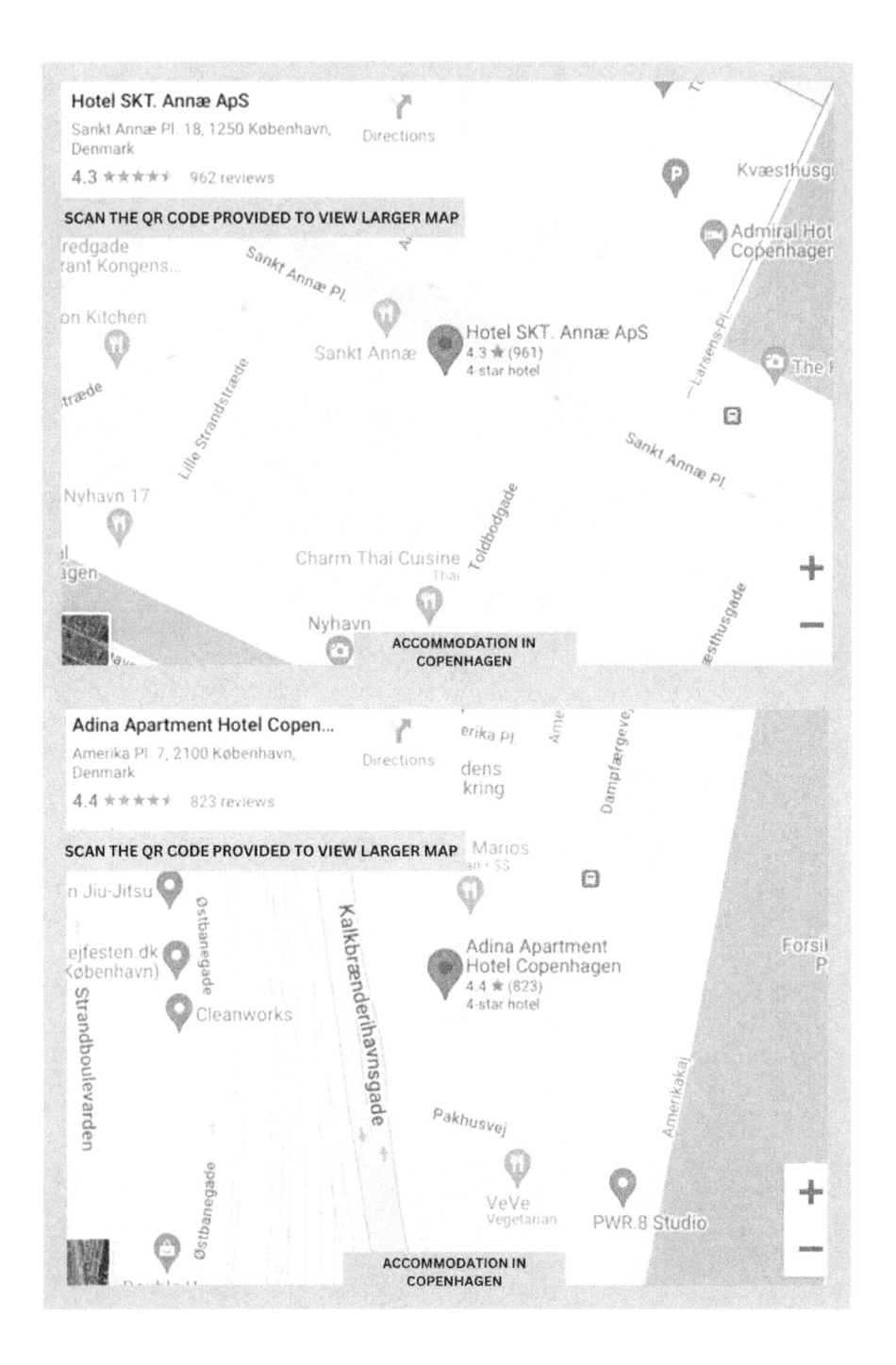

Hotel SKT. Annæ ApS
Sankt Annæ Pl. 18, 1250 København, Denmark
4.3 ★★★★ 962 reviews

SCAN THE QR CODE PROVIDED TO VIEW LARGER MAP

ACCOMMODATION IN COPENHAGEN

Adina Apartment Hotel Copen...
Amerika Pl. 7, 2100 København, Denmark
4.4 ★★★★ 823 reviews

SCAN THE QR CODE PROVIDED TO VIEW LARGER MAP

ACCOMMODATION IN COPENHAGEN

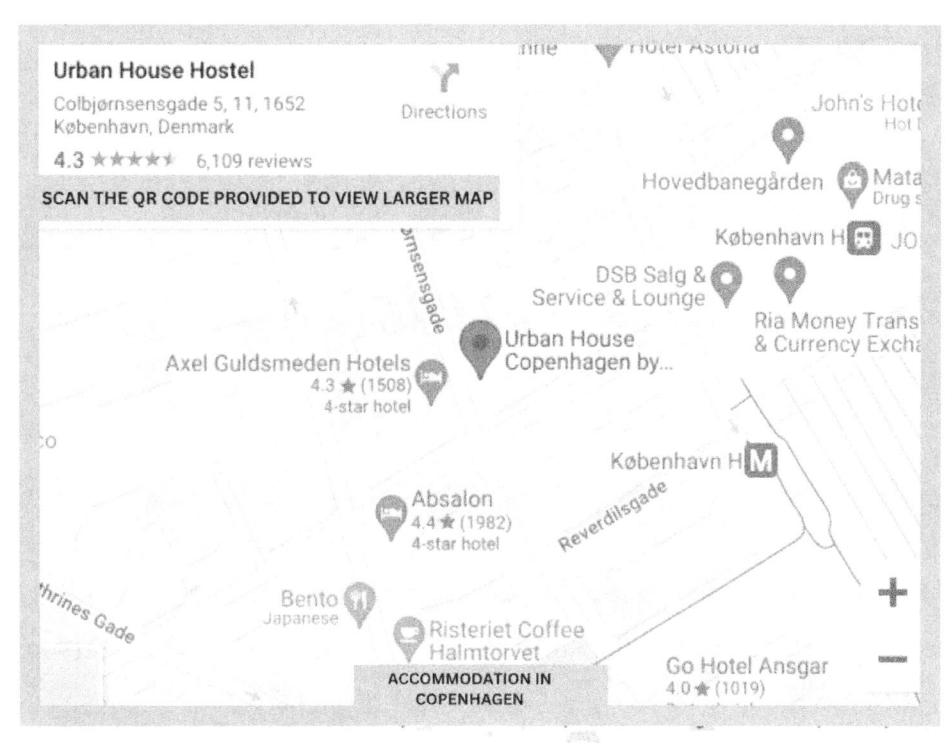

Urban House Hostel
Colbjørnsensgade 5, 11, 1652
København, Denmark
4.3 ★★★★★ 6,109 reviews

SCAN THE QR CODE PROVIDED TO VIEW LARGER MAP

ACCOMMODATION IN COPENHAGEN

Scan the QR Code with a device to view a comprehensive and larger map of Accommodation options in Copenhagen

2.1 Hotels in Central Copenhagen

Right from opulent grandeur to sleek contemporary design, these establishments offer a glimpse into the luxury and comfort awaiting those who seek refuge in the vibrant heart of the Danish capital.

Hotel d'Angleterre: Grandeur and Elegance

Located in the heart of Copenhagen's historic district, Hotel d'Angleterre exudes timeless elegance and sophistication. Situated on Kongens Nytorv, one of the city's most prestigious squares, this iconic hotel boasts lavish accommodations, impeccable service, and unparalleled views of the Royal Danish Theatre. Prices for lodging at Hotel d'Angleterre typically range from $300 to $800 per night, depending on the room category and season. Meal prices at Hotel d'Angleterre vary depending on the dining venue and menu selection, with breakfast starting at $30 per person and dinner at Marchal averaging $150 per person. For reservations and bookings, visitors can visit the official website at www.dangleterre.com.

Nobis Hotel Copenhagen: Contemporary Chic

Embrace modern luxury at Nobis Hotel Copenhagen, a sleek and stylish retreat nestled in the heart of the city's cultural district. Located on Niels Brocks Gade, just steps away from the iconic Tivoli Gardens, this boutique hotel offers a blend of Scandinavian design and international flair. Prices for lodging at Nobis Hotel Copenhagen typically range from $200 to $500 per night, depending on the room category and season. Special services at Nobis Hotel Copenhagen include bespoke concierge assistance, private dining options, and VIP airport transfers. Meal prices vary depending on the dining venue and menu selection, with breakfast starting at $25 per person and dinner at the hotel's restaurant averaging $100 per person. For reservations and bookings, visitors can visit the official website at www.nobishotel.com.

Hotel Sanders: Boutique Luxury

Experience the epitome of boutique luxury at Hotel Sanders, a charming oasis tucked away in the heart of Copenhagen's historic Latin Quarter. Situated on Tordenskjoldsgade, just a stone's throw from the picturesque Nyhavn harbor, this intimate hotel offers a haven of comfort and style. Prices for lodging at Hotel Sanders typically range from $250 to $600 per night, depending on the room category and season. Services at Hotel Sanders include private guided tours of Copenhagen's hidden gems, bespoke culinary experiences, and in-room spa treatments. Meal prices vary depending on the dining venue and menu selection, with breakfast starting at $20 per person and dinner at the hotel's restaurant averaging $80 per person. For reservations and bookings, visitors can visit the official website at www.hotelsanders.com.

Hotel Skt. Petri: Urban Oasis

Escape to an urban oasis at Hotel Skt. Petri, a chic retreat nestled in the heart of Copenhagen's vibrant Latin Quarter. Located on Krystalgade, just steps away from the iconic Round Tower, this stylish hotel offers a blend of contemporary design and historic charm. Prices for lodging at Hotel Skt. Petri typically range from $200 to $500 per night, depending on the room category and season. Services at Hotel Skt. Petri include personalized concierge assistance, private dining options, and VIP access to local attractions and events. Meal prices vary depending on the dining venue and menu selection, with breakfast starting at $25 per person and dinner at the hotel's restaurant averaging $100 per person. For reservations and bookings, visitors can visit the official website at www.hotelsktpetri.com.

2.2 Budget-Friendly Hostels and Guesthouses

Exploring Copenhagen on a budget doesn't mean sacrificing comfort or charm, especially when you have an array of budget-friendly hostels and guesthouses waiting to welcome you with open arms. Join me as we discover various unique and wallet-friendly options for lodging in Copenhagen, each offering its own blend of affordability, convenience, and hospitality.

Urban House Copenhagen by MEININGER

Located in the vibrant Vesterbro district, Urban House Copenhagen by MEININGER offers a modern and eclectic atmosphere for budget-conscious travelers. With dormitory-style rooms starting at just €20 per night, this hostel provides comfortable accommodations without breaking the bank. Amenities include free Wi-Fi, a communal kitchen, and a cozy lounge area perfect for socializing with fellow travelers. Unique features include bike rentals and guided city tours, allowing guests to explore Copenhagen's hidden gems without emptying their wallets. Meals are available at an additional cost, with a variety of options to suit every palate. For bookings and reservations, visit their official website at www.meininger-hotels.com.

Generator Copenhagen

Situated in the heart of the city near Kongens Nytorv Square, Generator Copenhagen offers stylish and affordable lodging for budget travelers. Dormitory beds start at €25 per night, making it an ideal choice for those seeking comfort on a budget. The hostel boasts a lively social atmosphere, with a bar and lounge area serving up cocktails and live music. Additional amenities include free Wi-Fi, laundry facilities, and 24-hour reception. Unique features include an onsite travel desk offering guided tours and excursions, allowing guests to explore Copenhagen's top attractions with ease. For those craving a bite to eat, the hostel's café offers a range of affordable meal options. To book your stay, visit their official website at www.generatorhostels.com.

Copenhagen Downtown Hostel

Copenhagen Downtown Hostel offers affordable accommodations with a laid-back and friendly vibe. Dormitory beds start at €20 per night, making it a budget-friendly option for travelers of all ages. The hostel features a communal kitchen, free Wi-Fi, and a cozy lounge area perfect for mingling with fellow guests. Unique features include themed events and activities, such as movie nights and pub crawls, providing ample opportunities for socializing and making new friends. For those looking to explore the city on a budget, the hostel offers bike rentals at competitive rates. Guests can also enjoy affordable meals at the onsite café, serving up delicious Danish fare. For reservations and more information, visit their official website at www.copenhagendowntown.com.

Bedwood Hostel

Tucked away in the charming neighborhood of Frederiksberg, Bedwood Hostel offers a cozy and intimate atmosphere for budget travelers seeking a home away from home. Dormitory beds start at €18 per night, making it one of the most affordable options in Copenhagen. The hostel features a communal kitchen, free Wi-Fi, and a cozy lounge area complete with board games and books. Unique features include themed décor inspired by Danish design, giving guests a taste of local culture and heritage. For those seeking a taste of authentic Danish cuisine, the hostel offers a complimentary breakfast buffet each morning. Additional services include bike rentals and luggage storage, ensuring a hassle-free stay for guests. To book your stay, visit their official website at www.bedwoodhostel.dk.

Woodah Hostel

Located in the trendy Nørrebro district, Woodah Hostel offers eco-friendly accommodations with a focus on sustainability and community. Dormitory beds start at €22 per night, making it an affordable option for environmentally conscious travelers. The hostel features recycled and upcycled furnishings, solar panels, and composting facilities, allowing guests to minimize their carbon footprint while enjoying a comfortable stay. Amenities include a communal kitchen, free Wi-Fi, and a cozy outdoor courtyard perfect for soaking up the sun. Unique features include yoga classes and workshops on sustainability, providing guests with opportunities to connect with like-minded travelers and learn new skills. For bookings and reservations, visit their official website at www.woodah-hostel.com.

Budget-friendly accommodations in Copenhagen offer more than just a place to rest your head, they provide an opportunity to immerse yourself in the city's vibrant culture, forge connections with fellow travelers, and create unforgettable memories.

2.3 Boutique Hotels and Design Stays

Copenhagen, with its reputation for cutting-edge design, cultural sophistication, and impeccable hospitality, offers a plethora of boutique hotels and design stays that redefine the concept of luxury lodging. These establishments not only provide comfortable accommodations but also immerse guests in the city's unique charm and creativity. Here, we delve into exceptional boutique hotels and design stays that exemplify Copenhagen's flair for style and hospitality.

Hotel SP34

Located in the vibrant Latin Quarter of Copenhagen, Hotel SP34 stands out as a beacon of contemporary design and urban luxury. This boutique hotel seamlessly blends modern aesthetics with historic charm, offering guests a truly unique experience. With its central location, guests have easy access to iconic attractions such as Tivoli Gardens, Nyhavn Harbor, and the Royal Danish Theatre.

Hotel SP34 boasts a range of room options, from cozy single rooms to spacious suites, each meticulously designed with Scandinavian minimalism and comfort in mind. Prices for lodging start at approximately $200 per night, making it an accessible yet indulgent choice for travelers. Guests can enjoy a host of amenities, including complimentary Wi-Fi, a fitness center, and a stylish rooftop terrace with panoramic views of the city skyline. The hotel's unique feature is its emphasis on sustainability, with eco-friendly initiatives implemented throughout the property. For more information and reservations, visit the official website: (https://www.brochner-hotels.com/hotel-sp34/)

Nobis Hotel Copenhagen

Nobis Hotel Copenhagen exudes timeless elegance and sophistication. Housed in a former 5-star deluxe hotel, this boutique establishment offers a seamless blend of classic architecture and contemporary design. Guests can choose from a range of luxurious rooms and suites, each elegantly appointed with modern amenities and plush furnishings. Prices for lodging at Nobis Hotel Copenhagen start at approximately $300 per night, reflecting the hotel's upscale ambiance and premium offerings. For bookings and reservations, visit the official website: (https://nobishotel.dk/)

71 Nyhavn Hotel

Situated along the picturesque waterfront of Nyhavn Harbor, 71 Nyhavn Hotel occupies a historic warehouse building dating back to the 1800s. This charming boutique hotel offers guests a glimpse into Copenhagen's maritime heritage while providing modern comforts and amenities. The hotel features a range of beautifully appointed rooms and suites, many offering stunning views of the harbor and colorful facades of Nyhavn. Prices for lodging at 71 Nyhavn Hotel start at approximately $250 per night, reflecting its prime location and waterfront ambiance. For bookings and reservations, visit the official website: (https://www.71nyhavnhotel.com/)

Hotel Alexandra

For travelers seeking a boutique hotel that celebrates Danish design heritage, Hotel Alexandra is the perfect choice. Located in the heart of Copenhagen's vibrant city center, this unique hotel pays homage to iconic Danish furniture designers such as Arne Jacobsen, Finn Juhl, and Hans J. Wegner. Guests can choose from a selection of individually decorated rooms and suites, each showcasing classic Danish furniture pieces and design elements. Prices for lodging at Hotel Alexandra start at approximately $150 per night, offering excellent value for discerning travelers. Amenities at Hotel Alexandra include a cozy lounge area, bicycle rentals, and a curated selection of design books and magazines for guests to enjoy. For more information and reservations, visit the official website: (https://www.hotelalexandra.dk/)

Manon Les Suites Guldsmeden

In the trendy Vesterbro district of Copenhagen, Manon Les Suites Guldsmeden is a boutique hotel that epitomizes bohemian chic and sustainable luxury. Inspired by exotic travels and global influences, this eco-conscious hotel offers guests a serene oasis amidst the bustling city. The hotel features a range of spacious suites and penthouses, each adorned with natural materials, lush greenery, and eclectic furnishings. Prices for lodging at Manon Les Suites Guldsmeden start at approximately $200 per night, reflecting the hotel's commitment to sustainability and comfort. For more information and reservations, visit the official website: (https://www.guldsmedenhotels.com/manon-les-suites-guldsmeden)

Copenhagen's boutique hotels and design stays offer a diverse range of accommodations, each providing a unique blend of style, comfort, and hospitality. Whether seeking historic charm, contemporary luxury, or eco-conscious living, visitors to Copenhagen are sure to find the perfect boutique hotel to suit their preferences and elevate their travel experience.

2.4 Apartment Rentals and Airbnb Options

In the bustling city of Copenhagen, apartment rentals and Airbnb options provide visitors with the opportunity to immerse themselves in the local culture and lifestyle while enjoying the comforts of home. These accommodations offer a diverse range of choices, from cozy lofts in the heart of the city to spacious apartments with scenic views of the waterfront. Here, we explore unique apartment rentals and Airbnb options that cater to different preferences and budgets, ensuring a memorable and personalized stay experience in Copenhagen.

Airbnb: Charming Loft in Christianshavn

For travelers seeking a cozy and character-filled accommodation in Copenhagen, this charming loft in Christianshavn offers the perfect retreat. Located in one of Copenhagen's most picturesque neighborhoods, known for its historic canals, colorful townhouses, and bohemian atmosphere, this Airbnb option provides guests with a unique and authentic Danish experience. The loft features a spacious open-plan layout, with exposed wooden beams, large windows, and stylish Scandinavian furnishings. Prices for lodging at this charming loft in Christianshavn start at approximately $150 per night, offering excellent value for couples or solo travelers looking for a cozy retreat in Copenhagen. For more information and reservations, visit the Airbnb listing: (https://www.airbnb.com/rooms/)

Nordic Housing Apartment Rentals

Nordic Housing offers a range of stylish and contemporary apartment rentals in Copenhagen, catering to travelers seeking upscale accommodations with modern amenities and personalized service. Located in various neighborhoods throughout the city, Nordic Housing apartments provide guests with the freedom and flexibility to live like locals while enjoying the comforts of home. For more information and reservations, visit the official website: (https://www.nordichousing.dk/)

Airbnb: Waterfront Penthouse in Islands Brygge

For travelers seeking luxury and sophistication in Copenhagen, this waterfront penthouse in Islands Brygge offers an unparalleled stay experience. Situated along the banks of the harbor, with panoramic views of the water and city skyline, this Airbnb option combines modern elegance with breathtaking vistas. Prices for lodging at this waterfront penthouse in Islands Brygge start at approximately $300 per night, reflecting its premium location and upscale amenities. For more information and reservations, visit the Airbnb listing: (https://www.airbnb.com/rooms/)

Copenhagen's apartment rentals and Airbnb options offer a diverse range of accommodations, each providing guests with a unique and personalized stay experience. Visitors to Copenhagen are sure to find the perfect home away from home to suit their preferences and enhance their travel experience.

2.5 Unique Accommodations: Houseboats and Eco-Friendly Stays

Exploring the enchanting city of Copenhagen, nestled in the heart of Denmark, offers a plethora of experiences for the adventurous traveler. Amidst its picturesque canals and vibrant culture, lies a unique opportunity to indulge in unconventional accommodations that blend seamlessly with the city's eco-conscious ethos. Houseboats and eco-friendly stays beckon visitors to immerse themselves in sustainable luxury, offering a distinctive way to experience Copenhagen's charm. In this essay, we delve into captivating options, each offering a distinctive allure, ranging from serene houseboats to innovative eco-friendly lodgings.

Copenhagen Houseboat: Nestled along the tranquil waters of Copenhagen's canals, the Copenhagen Houseboat offers a truly unique lodging experience. These charming houseboats boast modern amenities, including cozy bedrooms, well-equipped kitchens, and panoramic views of the surrounding cityscape. Guests can unwind on the spacious decks, basking in the serenity of their floating abode. Prices for lodging start at $200 per night, varying based on the season and specific houseboat chosen. Additionally, guests can opt for a delectable meal package, featuring locally sourced ingredients prepared onboard. For those seeking a memorable stay with a touch of maritime charm, Copenhagen Houseboat promises an unforgettable experience. For bookings and reservations, visit their official website: (www.copenhagenhouseboat.com).

Green Lighthouse: Situated in the heart of Copenhagen, the Green Lighthouse stands as a beacon of sustainable architecture and hospitality. This eco-friendly accommodation blends cutting-edge design with environmentally conscious principles, offering guests a guilt-free stay without compromising on comfort. The Green Lighthouse features energy-efficient amenities, recycled materials, and a minimalist aesthetic that emphasizes sustainability. Prices for lodging start at $150 per night, with options for single or double occupancy. In addition to its eco-friendly features, the Green Lighthouse offers bicycle rentals, allowing guests to explore the city in an environmentally friendly manner. For a truly green getaway in Copenhagen, look no further than the Green Lighthouse. For bookings and reservations, visit their official website: (www.greenlighthouse.dk).

Nyhavn Floating Hotel: Embracing Copenhagen's maritime heritage, the Nyhavn Floating Hotel offers a one-of-a-kind stay in the iconic Nyhavn district. These elegantly appointed floating accommodations provide guests with unparalleled views of the bustling waterfront, dotted with colorful townhouses and historic ships. Each room features modern amenities, plush furnishings, and nautical-inspired decor, ensuring a comfortable and memorable stay. Prices for lodging start at $250 per night, with options for deluxe suites available. Guests can indulge in gourmet dining experiences at the hotel's waterfront restaurant, serving up delectable Danish cuisine with a modern twist. For a quintessentially Copenhagen experience, the Nyhavn Floating Hotel offers charm, elegance, and a dash of maritime magic. For bookings and reservations, visit their official website: (www.nyhavnfloatinghotel.com).

Copenhagen Tree House: Tucked away amidst lush greenery, the Copenhagen Tree House offers a secluded retreat in the heart of the city. Perched high among the trees, these eco-friendly lodgings provide guests with a tranquil escape from the hustle and bustle of urban life. Each treehouse features rustic yet luxurious accommodations, complete with cozy beds, private balconies, and stunning views of the surrounding forest. Prices for lodging start at $180 per night, with options for treehouses of varying sizes available. Guests can partake in guided nature walks, yoga sessions, and eco-conscious workshops, immersing themselves in the beauty of their natural surroundings. For a harmonious blend of luxury and sustainability, the Copenhagen Tree House beckons travelers to reconnect with nature in style. For bookings and reservations, visit their official website: (www.copenhagentreehouse.com).

Urban Camping Copenhagen: For the adventurous traveler seeking a unique lodging experience, Urban Camping Copenhagen offers a refreshing alternative to traditional accommodations. Located in various parks and green spaces throughout the city, these eco-friendly campsites provide guests with the opportunity to immerse themselves in nature while still enjoying the comforts of urban living. Prices for lodging start at $50 per night for a tent rental, with options for additional amenities such as sleeping bags and camping equipment available. Guests can participate in outdoor activities such as hiking, cycling, and stargazing, making the most of their natural surroundings. For a budget-friendly and eco-conscious stay in Copenhagen, Urban Camping Copenhagen offers a memorable outdoor adventure. For bookings and reservations, visit their official website: (www.urbancampingcopenhagen.com).

Copenhagen's houseboats and eco-friendly stays offer travelers a myriad of opportunities to experience the city in a truly unique and sustainable manner. From serene houseboats to innovative treehouses, these accommodations blend modern luxury with eco-conscious principles, inviting guests to immerse themselves in Copenhagen's vibrant culture and natural beauty.

CHAPTER 3
TRANSPORTATION IN COPENHAGEN

3.1 Public Transport: Metro, Bus, and Train

Public transportation serves as the lifeblood of urban mobility, offering an efficient and sustainable means of commuting for millions of people worldwide. Copenhagen, the vibrant capital of Denmark, boasts an impressive public transportation network comprising metro, buses, trains, and other modes of transit, facilitating seamless travel for both locals and visitors alike. Understanding the intricacies of these systems and how to navigate them effectively can greatly enhance one's experience in exploring this captivating city.

Metro System

The Copenhagen Metro stands out as a modern and efficient mode of transportation, connecting key areas within the city and its outskirts. With its sleek design and punctual service, the metro offers a hassle-free way to navigate Copenhagen's urban landscape. Visitors can purchase single-ride tickets or opt for convenient multi-ride cards, such as the Rejsekort, which offers discounted fares for frequent travelers. The metro operates from early morning until late at night, ensuring accessibility throughout the day.

Bus Network

Complementing the metro system is Copenhagen's extensive bus network, which provides comprehensive coverage across the city and surrounding regions. From arterial routes to neighborhood services, buses offer flexibility and accessibility for passengers of all demographics. Travelers can utilize the DOT Mobilbilletter app to purchase tickets digitally or opt for traditional paper tickets available at kiosks and ticket machines. Additionally, Copenhagen's bus fleet includes environmentally friendly options, aligning with the city's commitment to sustainability.

Train Services

Denmark's renowned national rail operator, DSB, operates an extensive network of train services, connecting Copenhagen with various destinations across the country and beyond. Whether traveling to neighboring cities or exploring the scenic countryside, trains offer comfort and efficiency for long-distance journeys. Visitors can choose from a range of ticket options, including flexible fares and discounted passes for tourists. With frequent departures and reliable service, trains provide a convenient mode of travel for exploring Denmark beyond the capital.

Bicycle Infrastructure

In addition to conventional public transportation, Copenhagen boasts a renowned bicycle-friendly infrastructure, making cycling a popular choice for both locals and tourists. With dedicated bike lanes, ample parking facilities, and bike-sharing programs like Bycyklen, exploring the city on two wheels offers a unique and eco-friendly experience. Visitors can rent bicycles from numerous locations across Copenhagen or utilize the city's extensive network of cycling paths to navigate key attractions and scenic routes.

Navigating Copenhagen's Public Transportation

Effectively navigating Copenhagen's public transportation system requires a basic understanding of fare structures, routes, and service schedules. Visitors can plan their journeys using online resources such as the DOT Journey Planner or various mobile apps designed for public transit navigation. Additionally, information kiosks at major transportation hubs and stations provide assistance for travelers seeking guidance or recommendations.

Copenhagen's public transportation system exemplifies efficiency, accessibility, and sustainability, offering a reliable means of exploring the city's diverse attractions and surrounding regions. Whether by metro, bus, train, or bicycle, visitors can navigate Copenhagen with ease, immersing themselves in the vibrant culture and rich history of Denmark's capital.

3.2 Biking Culture and Bike Rentals

Copenhagen stands as a beacon of biking culture, renowned worldwide for its dedication to sustainable transportation and its extensive network of bike lanes. Embraced by locals and visitors alike, biking isn't just a mode of transportation here; it's a way of life. As you delve into Copenhagen's biking scene, you'll find a rich tapestry of experiences awaiting you.

Bike Rentals: Accessible and Convenient

Bike rental services in Copenhagen cater to the diverse needs of travelers, offering a range of options from traditional bicycles to electric bikes. One prominent rental service is "Bike Copenhagen with Mike," known for its fleet of well-maintained bikes and personalized service. Prices vary depending on the duration of rental, with daily rates typically starting around 100 DKK for a standard bicycle and 250 DKK for an electric bike.

Donkey Republic: The Go-To Bike Rental System

Donkey Republic stands out as a popular bike rental system in Copenhagen, offering a seamless experience for users. With numerous pickup and drop-off points scattered throughout the city, renting a bike with Donkey Republic is incredibly convenient. Users can locate and unlock bikes using the Donkey Republic app, eliminating the need for physical keys or paperwork. Prices are competitive, with hourly rates starting as low as 25 DKK for a standard bike.

City Bikes: Exploring Copenhagen's Landmarks

For those seeking a hassle-free biking experience, Copenhagen's city bike system provides an excellent option. Known as "Bycyklen," these sturdy bikes are equipped with GPS navigation and electronic locks, making them ideal for sightseeing adventures. Users can locate available bikes using the Bycyklen app and unlock them with a simple QR code scan. Prices are affordable, typically ranging from 25 DKK per hour or 120 DKK for a day pass.

Embracing the Cycling Lifestyle

Beyond mere transportation, biking in Copenhagen offers a profound sense of connection to the city and its culture. Joining a guided bike tour allows you to delve deeper into Copenhagen's history and landmarks while interacting with knowledgeable guides and fellow travelers. Companies like "Copenhagenize Design Co." offer engaging tours focused on urban cycling culture and sustainable city planning, providing valuable insights into what makes Copenhagen a global cycling capital.

In Copenhagen, biking isn't just a means of getting from point A to point B—it's a way to immerse yourself in the city's vibrant culture, explore its hidden gems, and connect with like-minded individuals. Whether you're renting a bike for a day of sightseeing or joining a guided tour to delve deeper into Copenhagen's cycling scene, you're sure to experience the city in a unique and unforgettable way. So, saddle up, embrace the two-wheeled lifestyle, and pedal your way through the enchanting streets of Copenhagen.

3.3 Taxi Services and Ride-Sharing Apps

Copenhagen, renowned for its efficient and eco-friendly transportation system, offers visitors a myriad of options to traverse the city's picturesque streets. Among the diverse array of transportation services available, taxi services and ride-sharing apps stand out as convenient and accessible modes of travel. Let's delve into five notable taxi services and ride-sharing apps that cater to the needs of both locals and visitors alike.

Uber: Revolutionizing Urban Mobility

Uber, a global leader in ride-sharing technology, has seamlessly integrated itself into Copenhagen's transportation network. With its user-friendly app interface, travelers can effortlessly hail rides to their desired destinations with just a few taps on their smartphones. Operating throughout the city, Uber provides a reliable and efficient means of transportation, ensuring prompt arrivals and comfortable rides. Whether you're heading to iconic landmarks such as the Little Mermaid or exploring the vibrant streets of Nyhavn, Uber's extensive coverage ensures convenience at your fingertips. For more information and to book your ride, visit Uber's website at www.uber.com

Taxa 4x35: A Trusted Local Choice

Established as one of Copenhagen's premier taxi companies, Taxa 4x35 boasts a fleet of well-maintained vehicles and experienced drivers, guaranteeing safe and reliable transportation services. With strategically located taxi stands across the city, including popular tourist hubs such as Tivoli Gardens and Strøget, Taxa 4x35 offers convenient access to transportation for visitors exploring Copenhagen's attractions. Whether you're in need of a quick ride to your hotel or seeking a guided tour of the city, Taxa 4x35's professional drivers are equipped to cater to your needs. To book a taxi or inquire about rates, visit Taxa 4x35's website at www.taxa.dk

Bolt: Affordable and Reliable Travel Solutions

Bolt, formerly known as Taxify, presents travelers with an affordable alternative for navigating Copenhagen's bustling streets. Offering competitive pricing and a wide range of vehicle options, including standard cars and eco-friendly hybrids, Bolt caters to various budgetary preferences without compromising on quality service. With its intuitive app interface and seamless booking process, Bolt ensures hassle-free transportation experiences for visitors exploring Copenhagen's diverse attractions. To book a ride or learn more about Bolt's services, visit their website at www.bolt.eu

Dantaxi: A Local Favorite

Dantaxi, synonymous with reliability and professionalism, has been serving Copenhagen's transportation needs for decades. With a reputation for prompt service and courteous drivers, Dantaxi remains a preferred choice among locals and tourists alike. Operating 24/7, Dantaxi offers round-the-clock accessibility, ensuring travelers can rely on their services regardless of the time or location. Whether you're arriving at Copenhagen Airport or exploring the city's vibrant nightlife, Dantaxi's fleet of vehicles stands ready to accommodate your transportation needs. For reservations or inquiries, visit Dantaxi's website at www.dantaxi.dk

GoMore: Empowering Community-Based Transportation

GoMore, a unique platform that connects drivers with passengers, offers a community-driven approach to transportation in Copenhagen. Through its ride-sharing services, GoMore fosters connections between travelers seeking affordable rides and local drivers with available seats in their vehicles. This innovative model not only promotes sustainable travel but also provides opportunities for cultural exchange and networking among participants. Whether you're commuting within the city or embarking on a day trip to nearby attractions, GoMore offers a flexible and cost-effective transportation solution for visitors exploring Copenhagen. To join the GoMore community or book a ride, visit their website at www.gomore.dk or download the GoMore app from the App Store or Google Play Store.

Copenhagen's diverse array of taxi services and ride-sharing apps cater to the varied needs of visitors, offering convenience, reliability, and affordability in navigating the city's attractions. Whether you opt for the global reach of Uber, the local expertise of Taxa 4x35 and Dantaxi, the affordability of Bolt, or the community-driven approach of GoMore, rest assured that you'll find a transportation solution that meets your preferences and enhances your Copenhagen experience.

3.4 Ferries and Water Taxis

Copenhagen's waterways offer a scenic and efficient mode of transportation, allowing visitors to explore the city from a unique perspective. With a variety of ferry and water taxi options available, navigating Copenhagen's canals and harbors is both convenient and memorable.

Copenhagen Harbor Buses: Seamless Waterway Transit

The Copenhagen Harbor Buses, operated by Movia, provide a convenient and efficient way to travel between key destinations along the city's waterfront. With multiple routes connecting popular attractions such as Nyhavn, the Opera House, and the Little Mermaid statue, these blue and white vessels offer a scenic alternative to traditional land-based transportation. Visitors can purchase tickets onboard or use the DOT Mobilbilletter app for easy fare payment.

Netto-Bådene: Quaint Canal Cruises

For a leisurely cruise along Copenhagen's picturesque canals, Netto-Bådene offers charming boat tours departing from Nyhavn. These classic wooden vessels provide a cozy atmosphere ideal for sightseeing and relaxation. Visitors can choose from various guided tours, including the Grand Tour, which covers major landmarks like Christianshavn and the Royal Palace. Tickets can be purchased online or at the ticket office located near Nyhavn's waterfront.

Haven Busserne: Harbor Explorations

Haven Busserne, also known as the Harbor Buses, provide hop-on-hop-off services along Copenhagen's waterfront, offering flexibility for visitors to explore at their own pace. Operating from spring to autumn, these green and yellow boats stop at key locations such as the Opera House, Black Diamond Library, and the Royal Palace. Tickets can be purchased directly from the onboard conductor, with discounts available for children and seniors.

Copenhagen Water Taxis: On-Demand Transportation

For a more personalized and direct mode of water transportation, Copenhagen Water Taxis offer on-demand services tailored to passengers' needs. These sleek black and yellow boats can be hailed from various locations along the waterfront or booked in advance via phone or online. Whether you're heading to a waterfront restaurant or seeking a quick transfer between attractions, Copenhagen Water Taxis provide a convenient solution. Pricing varies based on distance and time, with rates typically starting at around 200 DKK for short trips.

GoBoat: Eco-Friendly Canal Cruising

For those looking to captain their own vessel, GoBoat offers a unique and eco-friendly boating experience on Copenhagen's canals. These electric-powered boats accommodate up to eight passengers and can be rented by the hour, allowing visitors to explore the city's waterways at their own pace. No boating license is required, making GoBoat accessible to all. Reservations can be made online, with prices starting at around 450 DKK per hour, including fuel and life jackets.

Copenhagen's waterways via ferries and water taxis provides visitors with a memorable and convenient way to experience the city's maritime charm. With a variety of options to suit every preference and budget, navigating Copenhagen's canals becomes an adventure in itself, promising unforgettable moments and unique perspectives on this vibrant city.

3.5 Car Rentals and Driving Tips

Navigating Copenhagen by car offers travelers the freedom to venture beyond the city center and discover the surrounding regions at their own pace. With a variety of car rental options available, as well as essential driving tips to keep in mind, visitors can confidently navigate the Danish capital and its outskirts.

Avis Car Rental: Trusted Service and Reliability

Avis Car Rental is a well-established name in the industry, offering a range of vehicles to suit every traveler's needs. With multiple locations throughout Copenhagen, including at the airport and in the city center,

Avis provides convenient pickup and drop-off options. Visitors can book online through the (https://www.avis.com/en/home)

Hertz Car Rental: Worldwide Coverage with Local Expertise

Hertz Car Rental boasts a global presence and a reputation for quality service, making it a popular choice for travelers in Copenhagen. With several branches strategically located across the city, including at the airport and major train stations, Hertz offers easy access to rental vehicles. Booking can be done online through the website, (https://www.hertz.com/rentacar/reservation/)

Sixt Car Rental: Premium Vehicles and Flexible Options

For those seeking premium vehicles and personalized service, Sixt Car Rental delivers a high-quality rental experience in Copenhagen. With a diverse fleet of cars ranging from economy to luxury models, Sixt caters to discerning travelers' needs. Visitors can make reservations through the (https://www.sixt.com/car-rental/denmark/copenhagen)

Europcar: Affordable Rentals with Nationwide Coverage

Europcar offers affordable car rental options with nationwide coverage, making it an excellent choice for travelers planning to explore Denmark beyond Copenhagen. With multiple pickup locations in the city, including at the airport and central railway station, Europcar provides convenient access to rental vehicles. Reservations can be made online through (https://www.europcar.com/en/)

Budget Car Rental: Value for Money and Convenience

Budget Car Rental prides itself on offering value-for-money rentals with a focus on convenience and customer satisfaction. With several rental locations in Copenhagen, including at the airport and downtown areas, Budget makes it easy for travelers to pick up and drop off their vehicles. Booking can be done online through (https://www.budget.com/en/home)

Driving Tips for Navigating Copenhagen

While driving in Copenhagen can be a convenient way to explore the city and its surroundings, there are several essential tips to keep in mind:

-**Traffic Regulations:** Familiarize yourself with Danish traffic laws and regulations, including speed limits, road signs, and right-of-way rules.

-**Parking:** Pay attention to parking restrictions and signage when parking your rental car in Copenhagen. Utilize designated parking areas and pay-and-display meters to avoid fines.

-**Biking Awareness:** Copenhagen is renowned for its biking culture, so remain vigilant and watch out for cyclists when driving in the city. Give cyclists plenty of space and yield to them when necessary.

-**Toll Roads:** Be aware of toll roads and bridges in Denmark, which may require payment via electronic toll collection systems. Check with your rental company for information on tolls and how to pay.

-Navigation: Use GPS navigation or a map to navigate Copenhagen's streets and highways efficiently. Familiarize yourself with major landmarks and attractions to help orient yourself while driving.

By following these driving tips and choosing a reputable car rental provider, visitors can enjoy a smooth and stress-free experience exploring Copenhagen and its surrounding areas by car.

CHAPTER 4
TOP ATTRACTIONS AND CULTURAL HERITAGE

The Round Tower
Købmagergade 52A, 1150
København, Denmark
4.5 ★★★★★ 22,778 reviews

SCAN THE QR CODE PROVIDED TO VIEW LARGER MAP

TOP ATTRACTIONS IN COPENHAGEN

Tivoli Gardens
Vesterbrogade 3, 1630 København V, Denmark
4.5 ★★★★★ 78,113 reviews

SCAN THE QR CODE PROVIDED TO VIEW LARGER MAP

TOP ATTRACTIONS IN COPENHAGEN

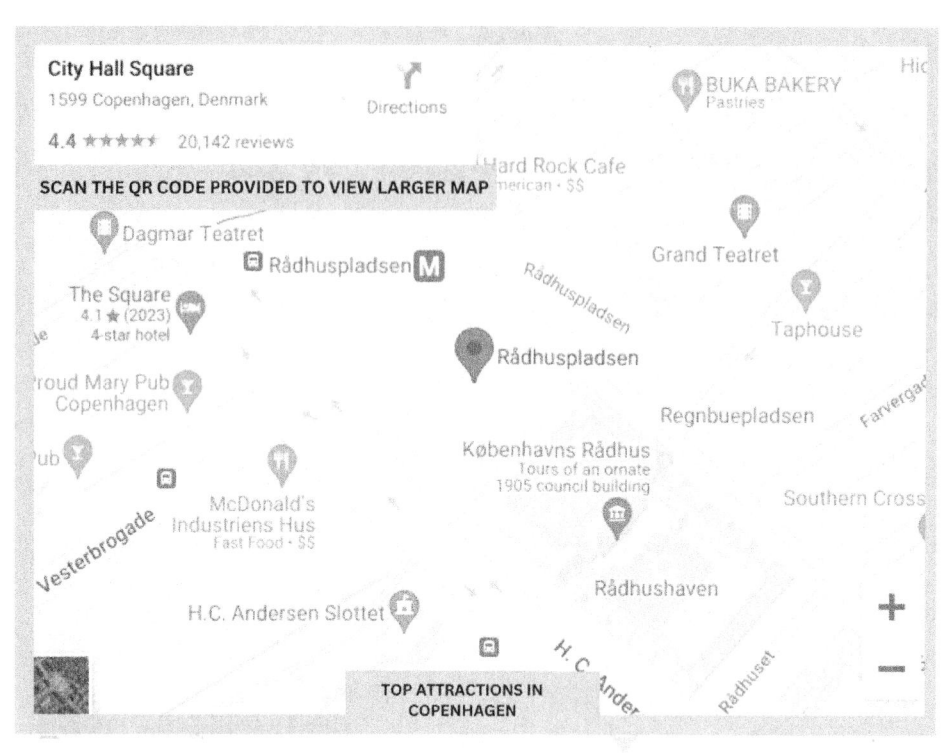

Scan the QR Code with a device to view a comprehensive and larger map of Top Attractions in Copenhagen

49

4.1 Tivoli Gardens and Amusement Park

Tivoli Gardens stands as a beacon of charm and adventure, captivating visitors from around the globe since its inception in 1843. Renowned for its timeless allure, Tivoli Gardens seamlessly blends the thrill of amusement park rides with the tranquility of lush gardens, offering an unforgettable experience for all who venture within its gates.

The Rutschebanen Roller Coaster

As one of the oldest wooden roller coasters in the world, the Rutschebanen Roller Coaster is a quintessential gem within Tivoli Gardens. Located in the heart of the park, this iconic ride promises an exhilarating journey through twists, turns, and gravity-defying drops. Its historic significance adds to the allure, as visitors can partake in a timeless tradition dating back to the park's earliest days. Thrill-seekers and history enthusiasts alike will find delight in this timeless attraction.

The Star Flyer

Standing tall as one of the tallest carousel rides in the world, the Star Flyer offers a bird's eye view of Copenhagen's picturesque skyline. Positioned at the edge of Tivoli Gardens, this towering attraction provides an adrenaline-pumping experience as riders soar through the air at dizzying heights. From the top, visitors can marvel at panoramic vistas of the city below, making it a must-see for those seeking both thrills and breathtaking scenery.

The Tivoli Concert Hall

Immerse yourself in the rich cultural tapestry of Copenhagen at the Tivoli Concert Hall, where world-class performances captivate audiences year-round. Nestled amidst the verdant gardens of Tivoli, this architectural gem serves as a hub for musical excellence, hosting a diverse array of concerts spanning classical, jazz, and contemporary genres. Whether attending a symphony orchestra or a lively jazz ensemble, visitors are sure to be enraptured by the enchanting melodies that resonate within this storied venue.

The Nimb Hotel

Step into a realm of luxury and refinement at the Nimb Hotel, an opulent oasis nestled within Tivoli Gardens. Housed within a historic Moorish-style palace, this iconic establishment exudes elegance and charm, offering unparalleled hospitality to discerning travelers. With its lavish accommodations, gourmet dining options, and impeccable service, the Nimb Hotel stands as a beacon of sophistication within the park, inviting visitors to indulge in a truly memorable experience.

The Tivoli Gardens Lake

Escape the hustle and bustle of the amusement park and bask in the serene beauty of the Tivoli Gardens Lake. Spanning across the heart of the park, this tranquil oasis provides a peaceful respite amidst the excitement of the surrounding attractions. Visitors can leisurely stroll along the lakeside promenade, marvel at the vibrant foliage reflected in the shimmering waters, or simply unwind amidst the idyllic scenery.

Whether seeking a moment of solitude or a romantic interlude, the Tivoli Gardens Lake offers a serene sanctuary for all who wander its shores.

Tivoli Gardens stands as a testament to the enduring allure of Copenhagen's cultural heritage, captivating visitors with its timeless charm and enchanting attractions. Whether embarking on a thrilling roller coaster ride, savoring gourmet cuisine at the Nimb Hotel, or simply basking in the beauty of the Tivoli Gardens Lake, there's something for everyone to enjoy within this iconic destination.

4.2 Nyhavn Harbor and Colorful Houses

Nyhavn Harbor is a vibrant kaleidoscope of colorful buildings, historic ships, and lively atmosphere that beckons travelers from across the globe. Nyhavn is more than just a harbor; it's a testament to Copenhagen's rich maritime heritage and cultural vibrancy. Upon arrival, one is immediately greeted by rows of impeccably maintained 17th-century townhouses, painted in an array of eye-catching hues that reflect in the tranquil waters of the canal. The iconic wooden ships docked along the quay add a touch of nostalgia, harking back to Nyhavn's days as a bustling commercial port. While there is no entry fee to explore Nyhavn itself, visitors may choose to embark on boat tours or dine at one of the many charming cafes and restaurants lining the waterfront.

Beyond its aesthetic allure, Nyhavn holds significant historical and cultural importance for Copenhagen. Originally constructed in the 17th century by King Christian V, the harbor served as a vital hub for trade, shipping, and commerce. Over the centuries, it evolved into a vibrant entertainment district, attracting artists, writers, and musicians who found inspiration amidst its picturesque surroundings.

Nyhavn remains a hub of activity, offering visitors a myriad of experiences to indulge in. From leisurely boat cruises along the canal to savoring traditional Danish cuisine at one of the waterfront eateries, there's something for everyone to enjoy. Additionally, Nyhavn plays host to various cultural events and festivals throughout the year, showcasing the city's rich artistic heritage. In essence, Nyhavn Harbor encapsulates the essence of Copenhagen's charm, seamlessly blending history, culture, and beauty into one captivating destination. Whether you're strolling along its cobblestone streets, enjoying a leisurely boat ride, or simply soaking in the vibrant atmosphere, Nyhavn promises an unforgettable experience that will leave a lasting impression on every visitor.

Colorful Houses: A Vibrant Tapestry of Architecture

Located within the iconic Nyhavn district, the colorful houses of Copenhagen stand as a testament to the city's architectural prowess and artistic flair. Stretching along the waterfront, these meticulously preserved 17th-century townhouses form a captivating backdrop to the bustling activity of the harbor. As visitors meander through the cobblestone streets of Nyhavn, they are treated to a visual feast of vibrant hues and charming facades. Each house tells a story of its own, with its distinct color palette and architectural style reflecting the unique personality of its occupants. From pastel pinks to bold blues, the houses of Nyhavn create a striking contrast against the tranquil waters of the canal, making for an iconic sight that has graced countless postcards and travel brochures.

Today, the colorful houses of Nyhavn serve as a symbol of Copenhagen's vibrant spirit and cultural heritage. Visitors can stroll along the waterfront, admiring the intricate details of each building, or stop for a photo against the backdrop of these iconic facades. The colorful houses of Nyhavn stand as a timeless testament to Copenhagen's architectural legacy and cultural richness. Whether you're a history enthusiast, an art lover, or simply a curious traveler, a visit to these iconic landmarks is sure to leave you inspired and enchanted by the beauty and charm of Denmark's capital city.

4.3 The Little Mermaid Statue

The Little Mermaid Statue stands as a timeless emblem of the city's charm and allure. While the statue itself is a must-see for any visitor, venturing into its surroundings unveils a treasure trove of iconic adventures and cultural heritage waiting to be explored. From historic landmarks to scenic landscapes, each destination offers a unique glimpse into Copenhagen's rich history and vibrant culture.

Kastellet: The Star-shaped Fortress

Located just a short stroll from the Little Mermaid Statue, Kastellet is a striking star-shaped fortress steeped in centuries of military history. Built in the 17th century, this well-preserved fortress is a testament to Denmark's strategic prowess and architectural ingenuity. Visitors can wander through its immaculately preserved ramparts, bastions, and barracks, immersing themselves in the atmosphere of a bygone era. Entry to Kastellet is free, making it an accessible destination for travelers of all budgets. From the statue, simply follow the waterfront promenade to reach this historic landmark.

Nyboder: The Historic Naval District

For a glimpse into Copenhagen's maritime heritage, venture into Nyboder, a charming historic district located just a stone's throw from the Little Mermaid Statue. Established in the 17th century to house the Royal Danish Navy, Nyboder is renowned for its iconic yellow row houses and picturesque cobblestone streets. Stroll through this quaint neighborhood, marveling at its colorful facades and tranquil atmosphere. While there is no entry fee to explore Nyboder, guided tours are available for those seeking deeper insights into its history and significance.

Amalienborg Palace: The Royal Residence

No visit to Copenhagen would be complete without a stop at Amalienborg Palace, the official residence of the Danish royal family. Situated within walking distance of the Little Mermaid Statue, this majestic palace complex comprises four identical rococo-style palaces surrounding an imposing statue of King Frederick V. Visitors can witness the changing of the guard ceremony, held daily at noon, or explore the opulent interiors of Christian VIII's Palace, which houses a museum showcasing the royal family's legacy. While entry to the palace grounds is free, there is a fee for guided tours of the interiors.

The Gefion Fountain: Myth and Majesty

Just a short stroll from the Little Mermaid Statue lies the Gefion Fountain, a breathtaking monument steeped in Norse mythology. Crafted in the early 20th century, this majestic fountain depicts the Norse goddess Gefjun driving her oxen across the sea, symbolizing the creation of the island of Zealand. Marvel at the fountain's intricate carvings and dynamic water features, and take a moment to appreciate its significance in Danish culture and folklore. Entry to the Gefion Fountain is free, making it a convenient stop for travelers exploring the area.

The Royal Danish Playhouse: Cultural Delights

For a dose of cultural enrichment, head to the Royal Danish Playhouse, a contemporary performing arts venue located along the waterfront near the Little Mermaid Statue. Designed by renowned architect Lundgaard & Tranberg, this striking building seamlessly blends modern aesthetics with traditional Danish design principles. Catch a world-class performance ranging from ballet to drama, or simply admire the building's sleek exterior and panoramic views of the harbor. While ticket prices vary depending on the event, the opportunity to immerse oneself in Denmark's vibrant arts scene is priceless.

The surroundings of the Little Mermaid Statue in Copenhagen offer a captivating tapestry of iconic adventures and cultural heritage waiting to be explored. From historic landmarks like Kastellet and Amalienborg Palace to artistic marvels like the Gefion Fountain and the Royal Danish Playhouse, each destination offers a unique glimpse into the city's rich history and vibrant culture.

4.4 Rosenborg Castle and Royal Residences

Rosenborg Castle stands as a beacon of regal splendor and cultural heritage, offering visitors a glimpse into Denmark's rich royal history. Built in the early 17th century by King Christian IV, this magnificent fortress-turned-palace has since become one of the city's most iconic landmarks, drawing travelers from far and wide to marvel at its opulent interiors and lush gardens.

The Royal Treasury

Step into a realm of opulence and grandeur as you explore the Royal Treasury of Rosenborg Castle. Located within the castle's hallowed halls, this treasure trove houses a dazzling array of regal artifacts, including priceless crown jewels, ceremonial regalia, and ornate coronation insignia. From glittering gemstones to intricately crafted goldsmithery, each piece bears witness to Denmark's storied monarchy, offering visitors a rare glimpse into the country's illustrious past.

The Knight's Hall

Immerse yourself in the medieval splendor of the Knight's Hall, where centuries of Danish history come to life amidst soaring vaulted ceilings and elaborately carved woodwork. Adorned with tapestries, suits of armor, and historic portraits, this majestic chamber serves as a testament to the chivalric ideals and noble heritage of Denmark's royal lineage. Visitors can embark on a journey through time as they wander amidst the hall's regal furnishings, imagining the grandeur of royal banquets and ceremonial gatherings that once took place within its walls.

The Royal Gardens

Escape the hustle and bustle of the city and wander amidst the verdant tranquility of the Royal Gardens at Rosenborg Castle. Spanning over 12 acres of meticulously manicured grounds, these lush green spaces offer a serene sanctuary amidst the urban landscape. Visitors can meander along winding pathways, admire colorful flowerbeds, and relax amidst shaded groves, soaking in the natural beauty and tranquility of this regal oasis.

The King's Chamber

Journey into the private quarters of Danish monarchs past as you explore the King's Chamber at Rosenborg Castle. Nestled within the castle's inner sanctum, this intimate chamber offers a rare glimpse into the personal life and regal opulence of Denmark's royal family. From ornate canopy beds to exquisite furnishings and portraits, each room tells a story of power, prestige, and royal privilege, inviting visitors to step back in time and experience the splendor of bygone eras.

The Rose Garden Pavilion

Indulge in a moment of tranquility amidst the fragrant blooms and elegant architecture of the Rose Garden Pavilion. Nestled within the heart of Rosenborg Castle's gardens, this picturesque pavilion serves as a charming backdrop for leisurely strolls and romantic interludes. Visitors can admire the vibrant hues of blooming roses, listen to the soothing sounds of trickling fountains, and revel in the timeless beauty of this enchanting sanctuary.

Rosenborg Castle stands as a testament to the enduring legacy of Denmark's royal heritage, captivating visitors with its timeless beauty and regal allure. Whether admiring its opulent interiors, wandering amidst its verdant gardens, or delving into its storied history, there's something for everyone to discover within the hallowed halls of this majestic fortress-turned-palace.

4.5 National Museum and Danish Design Museum

Copenhagen boasts a rich tapestry of cultural heritage, with its National Museums serving as beacons of history, art, and design. Among these gems, the Danish Design Museum stands tall, showcasing the nation's innovative spirit and artistic prowess.

Danish Design Museum: A Celebration of Creativity

Located in the historic Frederiksstaden district, the Danish Design Museum beckons visitors with its striking architecture and thought-provoking exhibits. As you step inside, you're greeted by a treasure trove of Danish design spanning centuries, from sleek furniture to avant-garde fashion. The Danish Design Museum transcends mere aesthetic appreciation; it offers a glimpse into Denmark's cultural identity.

National Museum: Preserving Denmark's Heritage

Situated in the heart of Copenhagen, the National Museum stands as a testament to Denmark's rich history and cultural heritage. Housed within a grand 18th-century palace, the museum invites visitors on a journey through time, from the Viking Age to the present day.

Getting to the National Museum is a breeze, thanks to its central location and excellent transport links. Whether strolling through the city streets or opting for public transit, reaching this cultural landmark is both convenient and rewarding.

Louisiana Museum of Modern Art: Where Nature Meets Creativity

A short journey from Copenhagen lies the Louisiana Museum of Modern Art, nestled amidst lush parklands overlooking the Øresund Strait. This architectural marvel seamlessly integrates art with nature, offering a serene retreat for cultural enthusiasts. More than just a gallery, the Louisiana Museum fosters a dialogue between art, architecture, and the natural world. Its ever-changing exhibitions showcase both established masters and emerging talents, inviting visitors to ponder, reflect, and connect with the world around them.

Ny Carlsberg Glyptotek: A Sanctuary of Art and Culture

Tucked away in the heart of Copenhagen, the Ny Carlsberg Glyptotek beckons with its neoclassical façade and verdant atrium. Founded by brewing magnate Carl Jacobsen, this museum boasts a diverse collection of antiquities and fine art. Inside the Ny Carlsberg Glyptotek, visitors are transported to distant lands and bygone eras, with galleries dedicated to ancient Egypt, Greece, and Rome. From marble sculptures to impressionist paintings, each exhibit offers a glimpse into humanity's enduring quest for beauty and meaning.

Thorvaldsens Museum: A Tribute to Danish Sculpture

The Thorvaldsens Museum pays homage to one of Denmark's most celebrated artists, Bertel Thorvaldsen. Housed within a majestic neoclassical building, the museum showcases the sculptor's masterpieces alongside artifacts from his life and times.

Copenhagen's National Museums offer an unparalleled journey through Denmark's cultural landscape, from ancient artifacts to cutting-edge design. Whether exploring the Danish Design Museum's innovative creations or marveling at the National Museum's historical treasures, visitors are sure to be captivated by the wealth of experiences awaiting them.

4.6 Hidden Gems: Off-the-Beaten-Path Discoveries

Nestled amidst the cobblestone streets and historic landmarks of Copenhagen lie a handful of hidden gems, waiting to be discovered by intrepid travelers seeking authentic cultural experiences beyond the well-trodden tourist trails. These off-the-beaten-path discoveries offer a glimpse into the lesser-known corners of the city, where history, art, and tradition converge to weave a tapestry of enchantment and intrigue.

Assistens Cemetery: A Tranquil Sanctuary of History and Remembrance

Tucked away in the vibrant neighborhood of Nørrebro, Assistens Cemetery stands as a serene oasis of greenery and contemplation amidst the bustling urban landscape. This historic burial ground, dating back to the 18th century, serves as the final resting place of numerous notable figures, including renowned Danish philosopher Søren Kierkegaard and fairy tale author Hans Christian Andersen.

Freetown Christiania: A Bohemian Enclave of Creativity and Community

Venture off the beaten path and into the eclectic enclave of Freetown Christiania, a self-proclaimed autonomous neighborhood nestled within the heart of Copenhagen. Founded in 1971 by a group of pioneering squatters, Christiania has since evolved into a vibrant hub of artistic expression, communal living, and alternative culture.

The David Collection: A Hidden Gem of Islamic Art and Culture

Within the historic confines of Copenhagen's Indre By district lies The David Collection, a hidden treasure trove of Islamic art, antiquities, and decorative objects. Founded by Danish lawyer and art collector C.L. David in the early 20th century, this exquisite museum offers a comprehensive overview of Islamic civilization spanning over a thousand years.

The Round Tower: A Renaissance Marvel with Panoramic Views

Rising above the rooftops of Copenhagen, The Round Tower stands as a testament to Danish ingenuity and architectural elegance. Built in the 17th century as an astronomical observatory and scholarly center, this iconic landmark offers visitors a unique opportunity to ascend its spiral ramp and enjoy panoramic views of the city skyline.

The Workers Museum: A Journey into Copenhagen's Industrial Heritage

Step back in time and uncover the hidden history of Copenhagen's working-class communities at The Workers Museum, a captivating cultural institution dedicated to preserving the legacy of Denmark's industrial past. Located in the vibrant district of Nørrebro, this immersive museum offers a fascinating glimpse into the lives of factory workers, artisans, and labor activists who shaped the city's social and economic landscape.

Beyond the well-known landmarks and tourist attractions, Copenhagen harbors a wealth of hidden gems waiting to be discovered by curious travelers. Whether wandering through historic cemeteries, exploring bohemian enclaves, or delving into the cultural riches of Islamic art and industrial heritage, each off-the-beaten-path discovery offers a unique opportunity to connect with the soul of the city and uncover its hidden stories and secrets.

4.7 Cultural Events and Festivals

In this journey of discovering the essence of Copenhagen, there is need to uncover iconic cultural festivals and events that define the city's identity and captivate the imagination of all who wander its storied streets. From the timeless charm of the Jazz Festival to the dynamic energy of the Distortion Festival, each destination offers a unique glimpse into Copenhagen's past, present, and future, inviting visitors to embark on a cultural odyssey like no other.

Copenhagen Jazz Festival: A Melodic Fusion

For lovers of music and culture, the Copenhagen Jazz Festival is a must-attend event. Since its inception in 1979, this renowned festival has celebrated the rich legacy of jazz while embracing diverse musical genres. Held annually in July, the festival transforms the city into a rhythmic haven for enthusiasts from around the globe. The Copenhagen Jazz Festival serves as a testament to the city's enduring passion for music and artistic expression. Rooted in the jazz traditions of New Orleans and Copenhagen's own vibrant scene, the festival fosters cross-cultural dialogue and collaboration.

Copenhagen Pride: Celebrating Diversity and Inclusion

In August, Copenhagen comes alive with a burst of color and camaraderie during Copenhagen Pride. Established in 1996, this annual celebration of LGBTQ+ pride and rights has grown into one of Europe's largest and most inclusive events of its kind. The festivities kick off with a vibrant parade that winds its way through the city center, uniting people from all walks of life in a joyous display of solidarity and acceptance. Throughout the week-long event, a diverse array of activities, including concerts, film screenings, and panel discussions, promote dialogue and awareness. Copenhagen Pride holds profound significance in Denmark's history of LGBTQ+ activism and advocacy. It serves as a platform for social progress and cultural exchange, fostering a more inclusive and tolerant society.

Copenhagen Fashion Week: Where Style Meets Innovation

For fashion aficionados, Copenhagen Fashion Week is a premier destination for sartorial inspiration and creativity. Established in 2003, this biannual event showcases the best of Scandinavian design while embracing global trends and influences. Taking place in February and August, Copenhagen Fashion Week attracts industry insiders, influencers, and fashion enthusiasts from around the world. The city's vibrant streets and historic venues serve as the backdrop for runway shows, presentations, and pop-up events. Copenhagen's reputation as a hub for sustainable and ethical fashion is reflected in the ethos of its fashion week. Many designers prioritize eco-friendly practices and social responsibility, shaping the future of the industry.

Copenhagen beckons visitors with a rich tapestry of iconic gems and cultural festivals that reflect the city's vibrant spirit and storied heritage. From the timeless charm of Tivoli Gardens to the dynamic energy of Copenhagen Fashion Week, there's something for everyone to explore and enjoy. Each experience offers a unique glimpse into the heart and soul of the city.

4.8 Outdoor Activities and Adventures

Copenhagen, often hailed for its cultural riches, also offers a plethora of outdoor activities and adventures, inviting visitors to explore its natural wonders and vibrant landscapes. From serene parks to scenic harbors, these outdoor attractions not only provide opportunities for recreation but also offer insights into Denmark's deep-rooted connection with nature.

Kayaking in Copenhagen: Paddling Through History

Exploring Copenhagen's waterways by kayak offers a unique perspective on the city's history and landmarks. With numerous rental companies and guided tours available, visitors can embark on a memorable journey through Copenhagen's canals and harbors. While some kayak rental companies charge a fee for equipment and guided tours, the experience of paddling past landmarks like the Little Mermaid statue and Christiansborg Palace is priceless. Additionally, exploring Copenhagen from the water provides insights into its maritime heritage and urban development.

Cycling Along the Harbor: Exploring Copenhagen's Maritime Heritage

Copenhagen's harbor area offers endless opportunities for outdoor exploration, with scenic bike paths winding along the waterfront. Renting a bike and pedaling through the harbor district allows visitors to soak in panoramic views of the city skyline and bustling maritime activity. To rent a bike, visitors can utilize Copenhagen's bike-sharing system or opt for one of the many rental shops scattered throughout the city. Once equipped with a bike, adventurers can embark on a self-guided tour of the harbor, stopping to admire landmarks like the Royal Danish Opera House and the colorful Nyhavn waterfront.

Picnicking in King's Garden: A Tranquil Retreat in the Heart of the City

For a peaceful escape from the hustle and bustle of urban life, visitors can head to King's Garden, the oldest and most visited park in Copenhagen. Located adjacent to Rosenborg Castle, this lush green space offers a serene setting for picnics, leisurely strolls, and cultural exploration. Getting to King's Garden is easy, with the park situated within walking distance of Copenhagen's major attractions and public transportation hubs. Whether arriving on foot, by bike, or via public transit, visitors can easily access this urban oasis.

Beach Day at Amager Strandpark: Sun, Sand, and Sea

Located just a short bike ride from Copenhagen's city center, Amager Strandpark beckons with its pristine sandy beaches and sparkling waters. Stretching along the coast of Amager Island, this expansive seaside park offers ample opportunities for sunbathing, swimming, and seaside recreation. While entry to Amager Strandpark is free, visitors should be mindful of any additional fees for equipment rentals or beachside amenities. However, the chance to unwind on Copenhagen's shores and soak up the seaside atmosphere is well worth the investment.

Copenhagen's outdoor activities and adventures offer a diverse array of experiences, from exploring historic parks to paddling along picturesque waterways. Whether embarking on a kayak tour of the city's canals or soaking up the sun on Amager Strandpark's beaches, visitors are sure to be captivated by the natural beauty and cultural significance of these outdoor attractions.

CHAPTER 5
PRACTICAL INFORMATION AND TRAVEL RESOURCES

Scan the QR Code with a device to view a comprehensive and larger map of Copenhagen

5.1 Maps and Navigation

While digital maps offer convenience and real-time updates, there's something timeless and reliable about a traditional paper map. Fortunately, Copenhagen is well-equipped with tourist information centers and kiosks that offer free or affordable paper maps to visitors. These maps typically highlight major landmarks, attractions, and key transportation routes, making them invaluable tools for navigating the city on foot or by public transport.

One popular option is to pick up a copy of the official Copenhagen City Map, available at tourist information centers, hotels, and select retail outlets. This comprehensive map provides detailed coverage of the city center, including major sights such as Tivoli Gardens, Nyhavn, and the Little Mermaid statue.

Digital Maps: Navigating Copenhagen in the Digital Age

In today's digital age, accessing maps on your smartphone or tablet has become second nature for many travelers. Copenhagen boasts a robust network of digital mapping services and apps that offer real-time navigation, interactive features, and personalized recommendations to enhance your exploration of the city. One popular digital mapping platform is Google Maps, which provides detailed street maps, public transport schedules, and walking directions for Copenhagen and beyond. Simply download the Google Maps app to your device, and you'll have access to a wealth of information at your fingertips, whether you're exploring the cobblestone streets of the Old Town or venturing out to the charming neighborhoods of Vesterbro or Nørrebro.

Comprehensive Digital Map: Click Here to Explore Copenhagen

For a comprehensive digital map of Copenhagen, we invite you to click on the link or scan the QR code provided in this guide. This interactive map offers detailed coverage of the city, including points of interest, dining options, shopping districts, and more. Whether you're planning your itinerary in advance or seeking inspiration on the go, this digital map will serve as your ultimate guide to Copenhagen's vibrant urban landscape. Navigating Copenhagen is an adventure in itself, with a myriad of options to suit every traveler's preferences and needs.

5.2 Essential Packing List

Whether you're exploring the colorful Nyhavn waterfront, visiting iconic landmarks like the Little Mermaid statue, or indulging in delicious Nordic cuisine, Copenhagen offers various experiences for travelers. To make the most of your visit, careful packing is essential. Here's a comprehensive guide to what you should pack for your trip to Copenhagen.

Clothing

When it comes to clothing, Copenhagen's weather can be unpredictable, so it's essential to pack layers. During the summer months, lightweight clothing like t-shirts, shorts, and dresses are ideal for exploring the city in the warm weather. However, it's advisable to pack a light jacket or sweater for cooler evenings or unexpected rain showers. In the spring and fall, a mix of both warm and cool weather clothing is necessary, including long-sleeved shirts, jeans, and a waterproof jacket. Winter in

Copenhagen can be cold, so pack warm clothing like heavy coats, scarves, gloves, and hats to stay comfortable while exploring the city.

Footwear

Comfortable walking shoes are a must for exploring Copenhagen's cobblestone streets and numerous attractions. Opt for sturdy walking shoes or sneakers that provide good support and are suitable for long days of sightseeing. If you plan to visit during the rainy season, waterproof shoes or boots are essential to keep your feet dry and comfortable.

Travel Accessories

Don't forget to pack essential travel accessories to make your trip to Copenhagen more enjoyable. A lightweight, water-resistant backpack or tote bag is ideal for carrying your belongings while exploring the city. Additionally, consider packing a reusable water bottle to stay hydrated throughout the day, as Copenhagen's tap water is safe to drink. A compact umbrella or rain poncho is also handy for unexpected rain showers.

Electronics

In today's digital age, electronics are essential for staying connected while traveling. Don't forget to pack your smartphone, along with a travel adapter and portable charger to keep your devices powered up. A camera or smartphone with a good camera is essential for capturing memories of your trip to Copenhagen's picturesque streets and landmarks.

Personal Care Items

Pack essential personal care items to ensure you stay fresh and comfortable throughout your trip. This includes toiletries such as toothpaste, toothbrush, shampoo, conditioner, soap, and sunscreen. Additionally, don't forget any prescription medications you may need, as well as over-the-counter medications for common ailments like headaches or allergies.

Travel Documents

Before you embark on your trip to Copenhagen, ensure you have all the necessary travel documents organized and packed securely. This includes your passport, visa (if required), travel insurance documents, flight tickets, hotel reservations, and any other relevant documentation. It's also a good idea to make copies of these documents and keep them in a separate location in case of emergencies.

Money and Currency

While credit and debit cards are widely accepted in Copenhagen, it's always a good idea to carry some local currency for small purchases or in case you encounter a place that doesn't accept cards. Danish Krone (DKK) is the official currency of Denmark, so make sure to exchange some money before your trip or withdraw cash from ATMs upon arrival.

Miscellaneous Items

Finally, consider packing a few miscellaneous items that can enhance your experience in Copenhagen. This includes a travel guidebook or map to help navigate the city, a reusable shopping bag for souvenirs and groceries, and a small first-aid kit for minor emergencies. Additionally, if you plan to indulge in Copenhagen's famous cycling culture, consider bringing a bike lock and helmet for safety.

Packing for a trip to Copenhagen requires careful consideration of the city's weather, culture, and activities. By packing essential clothing, footwear, travel accessories, electronics, personal care items, travel documents, money, and miscellaneous items, you can ensure a comfortable and enjoyable experience exploring everything this vibrant city has to offer.

5.3 Visa Requirements and Entry Procedures

For many visitors, the good news is that Denmark is part of the Schengen Area, which allows citizens of certain countries to enter without a visa for short stays. However, it's essential to check whether your nationality requires a visa for entry. If you do need a visa, you'll typically need to apply for a Schengen visa at the Danish consulate or embassy in your home country. The application process usually requires filling out forms, providing necessary documentation such as proof of accommodation and travel insurance, and attending an interview if required.

Customs and Immigration Clearance

Upon arrival in Copenhagen, travelers will proceed through customs and immigration clearance at Copenhagen Airport, Kastrup (CPH). Here, you will need to present your passport, visa (if applicable), and any supporting documents to immigration officers. Customs clearance involves declaring any items subject to duty or restrictions, such as alcohol, tobacco, or certain goods exceeding the duty-free allowance. Be sure to familiarize yourself with Denmark's customs regulations to avoid any delays or fines.

Entry Procedures by Air

Copenhagen Airport, Kastrup (CPH), serves as the primary gateway to the city and is one of the busiest airports in the Nordic region. Upon arrival, travelers will proceed through immigration control, where they may be required to present their passport, visa (if applicable), and any supporting documents.

Booking Flights

Booking flights to Copenhagen can be done through various channels, including airline websites, online travel agencies (OTAs), and travel comparison websites. These platforms allow travelers to compare prices, select preferred departure times, and choose seating options.

For direct bookings, travelers can visit the websites of the respective airlines. SAS (Scandinavian Airlines) offers a user-friendly booking interface, allowing passengers to customize their travel preferences easily. The website for booking SAS flights is (www.flysas.com). Similarly, other major carriers like Lufthansa (www.lufthansa.com), British Airways (www.britishairways.com) Air France (www.airfrance.com), and KLM Royal Dutch Airlines (www.klm.com) provide seamless booking experiences on their respective websites.

Entry Procedures by Train

Travelers also have the option of reaching Copenhagen by train, particularly from neighboring European countries such as Germany and Sweden. The EuroCity train connects Copenhagen with Hamburg, Germany, providing a scenic and convenient route for travelers. If arriving by train, passengers will undergo border control procedures upon crossing into Denmark. It's essential to have valid travel documents, including passports and visas if required, readily available for inspection by border authorities.

Entry Procedures by Road

For those opting to travel to Copenhagen by road, the city is well-connected via an extensive network of highways and roadways. Denmark is part of the European Union, allowing for seamless travel by car from neighboring countries such as Germany and Sweden. Upon entering Denmark by road, travelers may encounter border checks, although these are typically minimal due to the Schengen Agreement. However, it's still advisable to carry essential travel documents, including passports and vehicle registration papers, when crossing borders.

Whether arriving by air, train, or road, Copenhagen welcomes visitors with open arms, offering a wealth of cultural experiences, culinary delights, and architectural wonders to explore. By understanding the visa requirements and entry procedures, travelers can ensure a smooth and memorable journey to this enchanting Scandinavian city.

5.4 Safety Tips and Emergency Contacts

As you embark on your journey to explore the vibrant streets of Copenhagen, prioritizing safety is paramount to ensure a smooth and enjoyable experience. While Copenhagen is generally considered a safe city for travelers, it's essential to be aware of potential risks and take proactive measures to protect yourself and your belongings. In this guide, we'll outline essential safety tips and provide emergency contacts to help you navigate Copenhagen with confidence and peace of mind.

Stay Aware and Vigilant

While Copenhagen boasts a reputation for safety, it's still important to exercise caution, especially in crowded tourist areas and public transportation hubs. Stay vigilant of your surroundings and be mindful of pickpockets, particularly in crowded places such as Tivoli Gardens, Nyhavn, and the city center. Keep your belongings secure, avoid displaying valuables openly, and consider using a money belt or concealed pouch to safeguard your passport, cash, and credit cards.

Use Licensed Taxis and Transportation

When utilizing taxis or ride-sharing services in Copenhagen, ensure that you only use licensed operators to minimize the risk of scams or unauthorized fares. Licensed taxis display official signage and meters, and drivers are required to provide receipts upon request. Alternatively, consider using the city's efficient public transport system, including buses, trains, and the metro, which are safe and reliable modes of transportation for getting around the city.

Emergency Contacts: Who to Call in Case of Need

In the event of an emergency or if you require assistance during your stay in Copenhagen, it's essential to know whom to contact for help. Save the following emergency contacts in your phone or keep them handy for quick reference:

- *Police:* In case of criminal activity, theft, or emergencies requiring police assistance, dial 112, the universal emergency number in Denmark. The Danish police are highly responsive and trained to handle a wide range of situations, including medical emergencies and accidents.

- *Medical Assistance:* If you require urgent medical attention or medical assistance, dial 112 to reach emergency medical services (EMS) in Denmark. The EMS dispatchers are equipped to assess your situation and dispatch medical professionals to your location promptly. Additionally, Copenhagen boasts world-class healthcare facilities and hospitals, ensuring that you'll receive quality care in the event of illness or injury.

- *Embassy or Consulate:* If you encounter legal issues, passport loss, or require assistance from your country's diplomatic representation, contact your embassy or consulate in Copenhagen for support and guidance. They can provide consular services, including passport replacement, legal assistance, and emergency assistance for citizens abroad.

Stay Informed: Travel Alerts and Safety Updates

Before and during your visit to Copenhagen, stay informed about any travel alerts, safety updates, or advisories issued by your country's government or reputable travel advisories. These sources provide valuable information on potential risks, safety precautions, and local regulations that may impact your travel plans.

By following these essential safety tips and staying informed about emergency contacts and resources, you can enjoy a worry-free visit to Copenhagen and immerse yourself fully in the city's vibrant culture, history, and attractions. Remember to stay aware, use licensed transportation services, and keep emergency contacts readily available in case of need.

5.5 Currency Exchange and Banking Services

When preparing for a visit to Copenhagen, understanding the currency, banking options, and budgeting considerations is essential for a smooth and enjoyable trip. Denmark's official currency is the Danish Krone (DKK), often abbreviated as "kr." While credit and debit cards are widely accepted in Copenhagen, it's always wise to carry some cash for smaller purchases and in case of emergencies.

Currency Exchange and Banking Services

Copenhagen boasts numerous banks and currency exchange bureaus to cater to the needs of visitors. Among them, Danske Bank, Nordea, Jyske Bank, Sydbank, and Nykredit are prominent options offering a range of services to accommodate travelers.

Danske Bank has several branches across Copenhagen, including one at Copenhagen Central Station and another at Købmagergade. They provide currency exchange services and have ATMs widely available throughout the city.

Nordea is another major bank in Denmark with branches conveniently located in Copenhagen. Visitors can find Nordea branches at key locations such as Copenhagen Airport, Østerbro, and Frederiksberg. Nordea offers currency exchange services and provides assistance with various banking needs.

Jyske Bank is known for its personalized service and has branches in central Copenhagen, including one on Vesterbrogade. In addition to currency exchange, Jyske Bank offers tailored financial solutions for individuals and businesses.

Sydbank also has a presence in Copenhagen, with branches offering currency exchange services and banking assistance. One of their branches is situated at Nørreport Station, making it easily accessible for travelers.

Nykredit is a leading financial institution in Denmark, with branches in Copenhagen providing currency exchange facilities and banking services. Visitors can find Nykredit branches in areas like Nørrebro and Islands Brygge.

Budgeting Tips

While Copenhagen is known for its high standard of living, there are ways to experience the city without breaking the bank. Utilizing public transportation, such as buses and trains, can help save on transportation costs. Additionally, exploring local markets and eateries can provide affordable dining options while immersing yourself in Danish culture.

Currency Exchange Rates

Currency exchange rates can fluctuate, so it's recommended to check the current rates before exchanging money. While airport exchange desks offer convenience, they often charge higher fees compared to banks and exchange bureaus in the city center.

Copenhagen offers a range of banking and currency exchange options to accommodate visitors.

5.6 Language, Communication and Useful Phrases

Copenhagen boasts a population proficient in English, making it relatively easy for English-speaking visitors to navigate the city and communicate with locals. However, showing an effort to speak Danish or understanding some basic phrases can enhance your experience and demonstrate respect for the local culture.

Language

The official language of Denmark is Danish, a North Germanic language closely related to Swedish and Norwegian. While Danish may seem daunting to non-native speakers due to its unique pronunciation and pronunciation, most Danes are accommodating and appreciative of efforts to speak their language.

Useful Phrases

Learning a few basic Danish phrases can go a long way in making your interactions with locals more pleasant. Here are some useful phrases to know:

- *Hello: Hej (pronounced "hi")*
- *Goodbye: Farvel (pronounced "far-vel")*
- *Please: Vær så venlig (pronounced "ver sa ven-lee")*
- *Thank you: Tak (pronounced "tahk")*
- *Excuse me: Undskyld mig (pronounced "oond-skuel mee")*
- *Yes: Ja (pronounced "ya")*
- *No: Nej (pronounced "nai")*
- *Do you speak English?: Taler du engelsk? (pronounced "tah-ler doo eng-elsk?")*
- *I don't understand: Jeg forstår ikke (pronounced "yai for-stor ee-guh")*

Communication Tips

While English is widely spoken in Copenhagen, it's courteous to begin conversations with a polite greeting in Danish, such as "Hej" (hello), before switching to English. This gesture shows respect for the local language and culture. If you encounter someone who doesn't speak English fluently, speaking slowly and clearly can facilitate communication.

Cultural Considerations

In Danish culture, politeness and respect are highly valued. When interacting with locals, remember to use "please" and "thank you" liberally. Additionally, addressing people by their titles and using formal language, especially when meeting someone for the first time, is considered polite. For example, use "Hr." (Mr.) or "Fru" (Mrs.) followed by the person's last name.

Navigating the City

While English is prevalent in signage and public transportation announcements, knowing some basic Danish words can be helpful for navigating the city. For example, "Tog" means train, "Bus" is bus, "Metro" is metro, and "Gade" is street. Familiarizing yourself with these terms can make it easier to find your way around Copenhagen.

5.7 Shopping and Souvenirs

Fisketorvet Copenhagen Mall
Kalvebod Brygge 59, 1560
København, Denmark
4.2 ★★★★ 16,492 reviews

SCAN THE QR CODE PROVIDED TO VIEW LARGER MAP

SHOPPING OPTIONS IN COPENHAGEN

Welcome Giftshop & Souvenirs
Vesterbrogade 1h, 1620 København, Denmark
3.9 ★★★★ 15 reviews

SCAN THE QR CODE PROVIDED TO VIEW LARGER MAP

SHOPPING OPTIONS IN COPENHAGEN

Illums Bolighus Tivoli Hjørnet

Bernstorffsgade 3, 1577 København, Denmark

3.9 ★★★★ 64 reviews

Directions

SCAN THE QR CODE PROVIDED TO VIEW LARGER MAP

SHOPPING OPTIONS IN COPENHAGEN

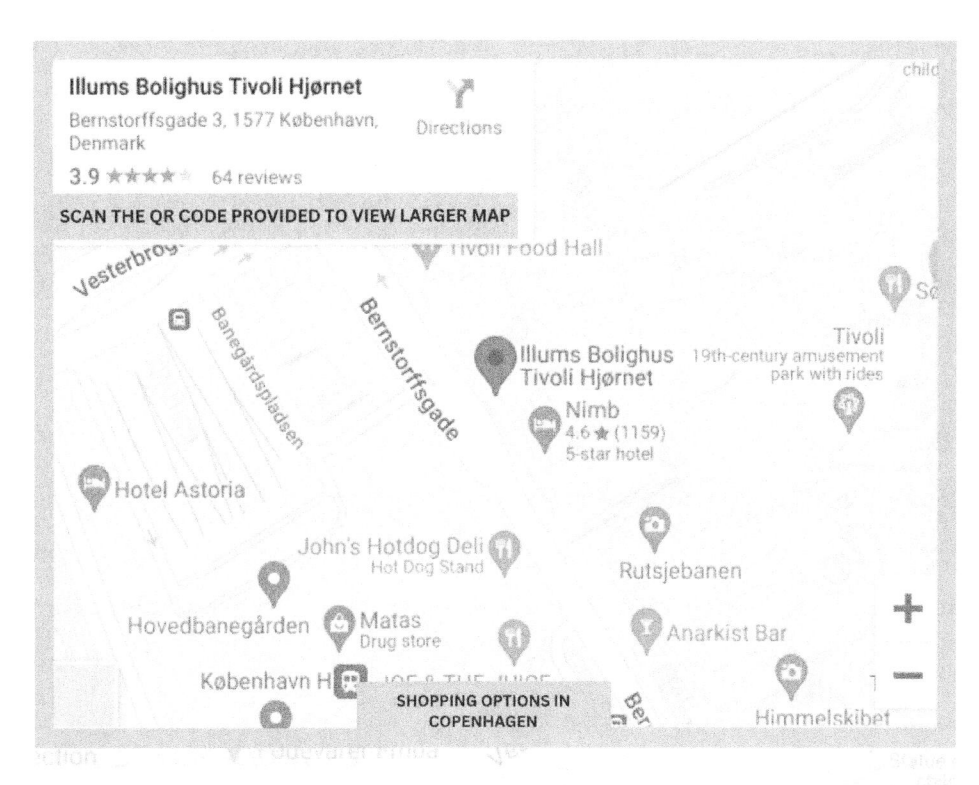

Scan the QR Code with a device to view a comprehensive and larger map of various Shopping options in Copenhagen

Exploring the vibrant streets of Copenhagen unveils a plethora of shopping delights, each offering a unique blend of culture, history, and craftsmanship. From boutique stores exuding contemporary elegance to antique shops resonating with the whispers of the past, the Danish capital boasts an eclectic array of shopping and souvenir options that cater to every taste and preference.

Boutique Marvels

Tucked away in the charming streets of Indre By, Copenhagen's historic inner city, lies the illustrious **Nordic Nest**. This boutique gem showcases a curated collection of Scandinavian design, ranging from sleek furniture pieces to exquisite home decor accents. Visitors can expect to find timeless pieces crafted by renowned Nordic designers, reflecting the region's minimalist aesthetic and impeccable craftsmanship. Prices vary depending on the intricacy of the design, with options suitable for both modest budgets and indulgent splurges. Nordic Nest typically operates from 10:00 AM to 6:00 PM, Monday to Saturday, providing ample opportunities for visitors to explore its treasures. Conveniently located near popular attractions such as Nyhavn and Amalienborg Palace, the boutique is easily accessible by foot or public transportation, ensuring a seamless shopping experience for discerning visitors.

Vintage Charms

Venturing into the eclectic district of Nørrebro unveils a treasure trove of vintage delights at *Retro Rehab*. Nestled amidst a vibrant array of cafes and galleries, this quaint antique store transports visitors back in time with its eclectic mix of retro clothing, accessories, and homeware. From funky 70s prints to timeless mid-century furniture, Retro Rehab caters to vintage enthusiasts seeking one-of-a-kind pieces to add character to their wardrobe or living space. Prices at this charming establishment are reasonable, offering budget-friendly options for thrifty shoppers and collectors alike. With flexible opening hours from 11:00 AM to 7:00 PM, Tuesday to Sunday, visitors can leisurely explore the store's nostalgic offerings at their own pace. Nørrebro's bustling atmosphere and artistic flair make it a must-visit destination for those craving a unique shopping experience off the beaten path.

Artisanal Treasures

For those seeking artisanal craftsmanship and local flair, a visit to *Illums Bolighus* is a quintessential Copenhagen experience. Situated in the heart of Strøget, one of Europe's longest pedestrian streets, this renowned department store showcases a curated selection of Danish design excellence across various disciplines. From handcrafted ceramics and glassware to contemporary fashion and accessories, Illums Bolighus celebrates the rich heritage of Danish design while embracing modern innovation. Prices range from affordable souvenirs to luxury investments, ensuring accessibility for visitors of all budgets. With extended opening hours from 10:00 AM to 8:00 PM on weekdays and 10:00 AM to 6:00 PM on weekends, the store accommodates both early birds and night owls alike. Conveniently located near major attractions such as Tivoli Gardens and the Royal Danish Theatre, Illums Bolighus is easily accessible by foot or public transportation, making it a must-visit destination for discerning shoppers.

Cultural Souvenirs

Immersing oneself in Copenhagen's cultural tapestry wouldn't be complete without a visit to *The Danish Design Museum Shop*. Located adjacent to the prestigious Designmuseum Danmark in Frederiksstaden, this charming boutique offers an extensive array of design-inspired souvenirs and gifts. From iconic Danish furniture replicas to quirky stationery and accessories, visitors can bring home a piece of Danish design heritage to cherish forever. Prices at The Danish Design Museum Shop cater to a wide range of budgets, with affordable trinkets and premium collectibles available for purchase. The shop typically operates during museum hours, from 10:00 AM to 6:00 PM, Tuesday to Sunday, allowing visitors to seamlessly integrate their shopping experience with a cultural excursion. Situated within walking distance of Amalienborg Palace and The Little Mermaid statue, the shop is easily accessible by foot or public transportation, ensuring convenience for cultural enthusiasts exploring the city.

Local Markets

For a taste of Copenhagen's vibrant street culture and culinary delights, a visit to *Torvehallerne Market* is a must. Nestled in the heart of Nørreport, this bustling food and flower market offers a sensory feast for visitors craving authentic local experiences. From fresh produce and gourmet delicacies to artisanal crafts and souvenirs, Torvehallerne Market showcases the best of Danish gastronomy and craftsmanship under one roof. Prices vary depending on the vendor and product, with options to suit every budget and palate. With early opening hours from 8:00 AM to 7:00 PM on weekdays and slightly reduced hours on weekends, the market accommodates both early risers and late shoppers. Conveniently located near Nørreport Station, one of Copenhagen's major transportation hubs, Torvehallerne Market is easily accessible by foot, bike, or public transportation, making it a bustling hub of activity for locals and tourists alike.

Copenhagen's diverse shopping landscape offers a myriad of opportunities for visitors to immerse themselves in the city's rich cultural heritage and contemporary flair. From boutique marvels showcasing Scandinavian design excellence to vintage charms echoing the whispers of the past, each shopping destination invites exploration and discovery.

5.8 Health, Wellness Centers and Safety Tips

Copenhagen, with its charming streets, vibrant culture, and dedication to sustainability, offers various options for maintaining health and wellness during your visit. From wellness centers focusing on holistic healing to safety tips for navigating the city, there's much to consider for a fulfilling and secure experience.

Embracing Holistic Wellness at Urban Healing

Nestled in the heart of Copenhagen, Urban Healing is a sanctuary for holistic wellness seekers. Offering a range of services such as acupuncture, massage therapy, and yoga classes, Urban Healing provides a holistic approach to health and well-being. Located at Vendersgade 12, this center is easily accessible and provides a tranquil escape from the bustling city life. Whether you're looking to unwind after a day of sightseeing or seeking relief from stress, Urban Healing offers a rejuvenating experience for both body and mind.

Rejuvenation at Serenity Spa

For those craving a luxurious escape, Serenity Spa offers a haven of tranquility amidst Copenhagen's urban landscape. Situated within the elegant confines of Hotel d'Angleterre at Kongens Nytorv 34, Serenity Spa boasts an array of indulgent treatments, from facials to body wraps, designed to pamper and revitalize. With its opulent ambiance and skilled therapists, a visit to Serenity Spa promises a blissful retreat from the rigors of travel, leaving you feeling refreshed and rejuvenated.

Mindfulness and Meditation at The Mindful Space

Incorporating the principles of mindfulness and meditation, The Mindful Space invites visitors to cultivate inner peace and harmony. Located in the vibrant district of Nørrebro at Jægersborggade 18, this wellness center offers guided meditation sessions, mindfulness workshops, and yoga classes to promote holistic well-being. With its welcoming atmosphere and emphasis on self-care, The Mindful Space provides a sanctuary for introspection and personal growth amid the bustling cityscape of Copenhagen.

Promoting Fitness and Well-Being at Copenhagen Athletic Club

For fitness enthusiasts seeking to maintain their exercise regimen while traveling, Copenhagen Athletic Club offers state-of-the-art facilities and personalized training programs. Conveniently situated at Øster Søgade 34, this fitness center provides a range of amenities, including cardio equipment, strength training machines, and group fitness classes. Whether you prefer a solo workout or guided instruction from certified trainers, Copenhagen Athletic Club caters to all levels of fitness, ensuring a rewarding and invigorating experience.

By embracing the offerings of Copenhagen's health and wellness scene while adhering to safety precautions, you can ensure a fulfilling and memorable visit to this enchanting city.

5.9 Useful Websites, Mobile Apps and Online Resources

Planning a trip to Copenhagen involves more than just booking flights and accommodations. Thanks to the digital age, there's a wealth of online resources, websites, and mobile apps available to help visitors make the most of their time in the Danish capital.

Transportation Apps

Navigating Copenhagen's public transportation system is made easy with apps like *Rejseplanen* and *DOT Mobilbilletter*. **Rejseplanen** provides comprehensive route planning for buses, trains, and metro, helping visitors efficiently navigate the city. On the other hand, **DOT Mobilbilletter** allows users to purchase and store digital tickets for public transportation, eliminating the need for paper tickets and making travel hassle-free.

Language Translation Apps

While English is widely spoken in Copenhagen, having a language translation app like **Google Translate** or **iTranslate** can still be useful for overcoming language barriers and communicating with locals. These apps offer real-time translation of text, speech, and even images, ensuring smooth interactions during your visit.

Accommodation Booking Websites

Finding the perfect place to stay in Copenhagen is made simple with websites like Booking.com and Airbnb. Booking.com offers a wide range of hotels, hostels, and guesthouses to suit every budget and preference, along with detailed reviews and ratings from previous guests. Alternatively, Airbnb.com provides a variety of unique accommodations, including apartments, houses, and even houseboats, allowing visitors to experience Copenhagen like a local.

Food and Dining Apps

Exploring Copenhagen's culinary scene is a must-do for any visitor, and apps like *Too Good To Go* and *HappyCow* can enhance the dining experience. **Too Good To Go** helps users find nearby restaurants and cafes offering surplus food at discounted prices, reducing food waste while allowing travelers to sample delicious meals on a budget. For vegetarian and vegan travelers, **HappyCow** is an essential resource for discovering plant-based eateries and vegan-friendly restaurants in Copenhagen.

Leveraging websites, mobile apps, and online resources can greatly enhance the planning and experience of a visit to Copenhagen. Whether it's navigating public transportation, discovering local attractions, overcoming language barriers, booking accommodations, or exploring culinary delights, these digital tools provide valuable assistance for travelers looking to make the most of their time in Copenhagen.

5.10 Visitor Centers and Tourist Assistance

For visitors exploring this charming Scandinavian destination, access to comprehensive tourist assistance and visitor centers is essential to make the most of their trip. Here, we explore diverse visitor centers and the array of services they offer to ensure a memorable and seamless experience in Copenhagen.

The City Hall Square Visitor Centre

Located in the heart of Copenhagen at the City Hall Square, this visitor center serves as a convenient starting point for travelers eager to explore the city. Staffed with knowledgeable personnel fluent in multiple languages, the center provides detailed information on attractions, accommodations, transportation options, and upcoming events.

The Copenhagen Airport Visitor Information Centre

For those arriving in Copenhagen by air, the Copenhagen Airport Visitor Information Centre offers invaluable assistance right upon arrival. Situated within the airport terminal, this center caters to international travelers, providing essential information on transportation, accommodation options, and sightseeing opportunities. Staff members offer guidance on navigating the airport, accessing public transportation, and obtaining city passes for convenient travel throughout Copenhagen. Visitors can also benefit from currency exchange services, luggage storage facilities, and assistance with lost or delayed baggage, ensuring a hassle-free transition from the airport to the city.

The Nyhavn Tourist Information Centre

Nyhavn district, known for its colorful waterfront houses and lively atmosphere, the Nyhavn Tourist Information Centre offers a charming setting to gather insights into Copenhagen's attractions. Here, visitors can enjoy panoramic views of the picturesque harbor while receiving personalized recommendations from knowledgeable staff members. The center provides information on nearby landmarks such as the Royal Palace, Amalienborg, and the Little Mermaid statue, along with suggestions for boat tours and canal cruises departing from Nyhavn. Additionally, visitors can learn about dining options, shopping venues, and entertainment hotspots in this historic neighborhood, ensuring an immersive experience in Copenhagen's maritime heritage.

The Christianshavn Tourist Information Centre

Situated in the eclectic Christianshavn district, renowned for its canals, cobblestone streets, and vibrant cultural scene, the Christianshavn Tourist Information Centre offers a gateway to this bohemian enclave. Here, visitors can explore unique attractions such as Christiania, a self-proclaimed autonomous neighborhood known for its alternative lifestyle and community spirit. The center provides insights into guided walking tours, bike rentals, and cultural events happening in Christianshavn, allowing visitors to delve into its rich history and artistic ambiance. Additionally, staff members offer recommendations for local cafes, galleries, and artisanal shops, enabling visitors to immerse themselves fully in the neighborhood's eclectic charm.

The Tivoli Gardens Visitor Centre

As one of Copenhagen's most beloved attractions, Tivoli Gardens boasts a dedicated visitor center catering to guests eager to experience its enchanting blend of amusement, culture, and entertainment. Located within the park grounds, the Tivoli Gardens Visitor Centre offers comprehensive assistance to ensure a memorable visit for guests of all ages. Here, visitors can obtain information on ride schedules, live performances, and special events hosted within the park, along with tips for dining options and souvenir shopping. The center also provides assistance with purchasing tickets, accessing VIP experiences, and arranging group outings or corporate events, making it an indispensable resource for experiencing the magic of Tivoli Gardens.

Navigating the cultural treasures and dynamic offerings of Copenhagen is made effortless through the array of visitor centers and tourist assistance services available throughout the city. From the bustling City Hall Square to the tranquil canals of Christianshavn, each center offers a unique perspective and invaluable support for visitors seeking to explore Copenhagen's diverse attractions. With personalized recommendations, practical assistance, and a warm welcome awaiting at every turn, travelers can embark on a memorable journey through the Danish capital, enriched by the insights and hospitality of its dedicated tourism professionals.

5.11 Recommended Tour Operators and Guided Tours

Exploring Copenhagen's rich cultural heritage, stunning architecture, and vibrant atmosphere can be greatly enhanced by joining guided tours operated by knowledgeable experts. Here are recommended tour operators and guided tours that offer comprehensive experiences for visitors to Copenhagen.

Copenhagen Free Walking Tours

Copenhagen Free Walking Tours is a popular choice for visitors seeking informative and engaging guided tours of the city. Led by local guides passionate about sharing their insights and stories, these tours offer a comprehensive overview of Copenhagen's landmarks, including the iconic Nyhavn, the historic Royal Palace, and the picturesque Little Mermaid statue. The tours typically last around two to three hours and operate on a pay-what-you-wish basis, making them accessible to all budgets.

Hey Captain Canal Tours

Tours depart from Nyhavn, specifically from Bådfarten's ticket office at Nyhavn 3, 1051 København K. For a unique perspective on Copenhagen's waterfront and architectural highlights, Hey Captain Canal Tours offers guided boat tours along the city's picturesque canals. Visitors can relax on board a comfortable boat while knowledgeable guides provide fascinating commentary on Copenhagen's history, culture, and landmarks. Highlights of the tour include passing by the colorful houses of Nyhavn, the modern architecture of Copenhagen Opera House, and the historic Christianshavn district.

Bike Copenhagen with Mike

For active travelers looking to explore Copenhagen's bike-friendly streets and scenic bike paths, Bike Copenhagen with Mike offers guided bicycle tours led by experienced local guides. Meeting point is at the bike rental shop located at Linnésgade 16, 1361 København K. These tours provide a unique opportunity to discover the city's hidden gems, including charming neighborhoods, green spaces, and cultural landmarks. From the bustling streets of the city center to the tranquil parks along the waterfront, participants can immerse themselves in Copenhagen's vibrant atmosphere while enjoying the freedom of cycling.

Stromma - Grand Tour of Copenhagen

Stromma offers a comprehensive guided bus tour of Copenhagen, providing visitors with an in-depth exploration of the city's main attractions and neighborhoods. the Stromma ticket office at Vesterbrogade 6D, 1620 København V. Led by experienced guides, the Grand Tour of Copenhagen covers highlights such as the Tivoli Gardens, the Amalienborg Palace, and the vibrant district of Christianshavn. With audio commentary available in multiple languages, participants can learn about Copenhagen's history and culture while enjoying panoramic views from the comfort of a bus.

Urban Adventures - Copenhagen Food Tour

For food enthusiasts eager to discover Copenhagen's culinary delights, Urban Adventures offers a mouthwatering food tour led by local guides passionate about Danish cuisine. The food market located at Frederiksborggade 21, 1360 København K. Participants can sample traditional dishes, artisanal snacks, and gourmet treats while exploring Copenhagen's food markets, bakeries, and eateries. From smørrebrød (open-faced sandwiches) to Danish pastries, this guided tour provides a delicious introduction to the city's gastronomic scene.

Joining guided tours operated by reputable tour operators is an excellent way for visitors to immerse themselves in Copenhagen's culture, history, and cuisine. With a variety of options available, ranging from walking tours to canal cruises to culinary experiences, travelers can tailor their exploration of Copenhagen to suit their interests and preferences.

CHAPTER 6
CULINARY DELIGHTS

6.1 Traditional Danish Cuisine: Smørrebrød, Frikadeller

Exploring the culinary landscape of Copenhagen unveils a delightful journey into the heart of Danish tradition and culture. Renowned for its simplicity, freshness, and emphasis on locally sourced ingredients, Traditional Danish Cuisine offers a rich tapestry of flavors that captivate both locals and visitors alike. Among the array of dishes that define Danish gastronomy, Here are quintessential examples of the country's culinary heritage. From the iconic open-faced sandwiches known as Smørrebrød to the savory meatballs called Frikadeller, each dish tells a story of tradition, craftsmanship, and a deep connection to the land.

Smørrebrød: A Culinary Canvas

At the forefront of Danish cuisine is the beloved Smørrebrød, a quintessential Danish dish that embodies simplicity and elegance. Consisting of a slice of dense rye bread topped with an array of flavorful ingredients, Smørrebrød is a culinary canvas where creativity knows no bounds. One can find this Danish delicacy served across Copenhagen, from traditional eateries to modern bistros. For an authentic experience, visit renowned establishments like Aamanns Deli & Take Away or Schønnemanns Restaurant & Bar, where you can indulge in classic variations such as herring with onions and capers, or roast beef with remoulade. Prices typically range from 60 to 120 Danish kroner per piece, depending on the toppings and the venue's ambiance.

Frikadeller: Danish Comfort Food

In the realm of Danish comfort food, Frikadeller reigns supreme. These flavorful meatballs, typically made from a mixture of ground pork and veal, seasoned with onions, nutmeg, and parsley, are a staple in Danish households and eateries alike. When in Copenhagen, head to traditional Danish restaurants like Restaurant Kronborg or Ida Davidsen, where you can savor Frikadeller served with creamy potatoes, tangy red cabbage, and a dollop of rich gravy. Prices for a hearty serving of Frikadeller usually range from 100 to 150 Danish kroner, making it an affordable and satisfying meal option for visitors seeking an authentic taste of Danish cuisine.

Æbleskiver: Delightful Danish Pancake Balls

For a sweet indulgence that captures the essence of Danish coziness, look no further than Æbleskiver. These delightful pancake balls, often enjoyed during the festive season or as a comforting treat on chilly days, are a beloved Danish tradition. Typically served with a dusting of powdered sugar and a dollop of jam, Æbleskiver can be found at traditional Danish bakeries such as Lagkagehuset or Andersen Bakery, where they are freshly prepared and served piping hot. Prices vary depending on the quantity and accompaniments, but a serving of Æbleskiver usually ranges from 40 to 80 Danish kroner, making it an affordable and irresistible indulgence for visitors exploring the streets of Copenhagen.

Stegt Flæsk: Danish Pork Belly Delight

Embodying the essence of Danish comfort food, Stegt Flæsk is a hearty dish that celebrates the rich flavors of pork belly. Thinly sliced and crisped to perfection, the pork belly is typically served with boiled potatoes, parsley sauce, and a tangy apple compote, creating a harmonious symphony of flavors and textures. When in Copenhagen, venture to traditional Danish eateries like Restaurant Schønnemann or Det Lille Apotek, where you can savor this iconic dish in an authentic setting. Prices for a serving of Stegt Flæsk typically range from 120 to 180 Danish kroner, making it a satisfying and affordable option for visitors seeking a taste of Danish culinary heritage.

Rødgrød med Fløde: A Taste of Danish Summer

No exploration of Traditional Danish Cuisine would be complete without a taste of Rødgrød med Fløde, a quintessential Danish dessert that celebrates the vibrant flavors of summer fruits. Consisting of a thick, berry compote served with a generous dollop of whipped cream, Rødgrød med Fløde is a refreshing and indulgent treat that delights the senses. While it may be challenging to find this traditional dessert in restaurants, visitors can experience the true essence of Danish hospitality by attending local summer festivals or farmers' markets, where Rødgrød med Fløde is often served fresh and homemade. Prices vary depending on the venue and portion size, but expect to pay around 50 to 100 Danish kroner for a serving of this delightful dessert.

Traditional Danish Cuisine in Copenhagen is a journey of discovery, where each dish tells a story of heritage, craftsmanship, and a deep connection to the land. From the iconic Smørrebrød to the comforting Frikadeller and the indulgent Rødgrød med Fløde, Danish cuisine offers a rich tapestry of flavors that captivates the senses and leaves a lasting impression on visitors.

6.2 New Nordic Cuisine and Michelin-Starred Restaurants

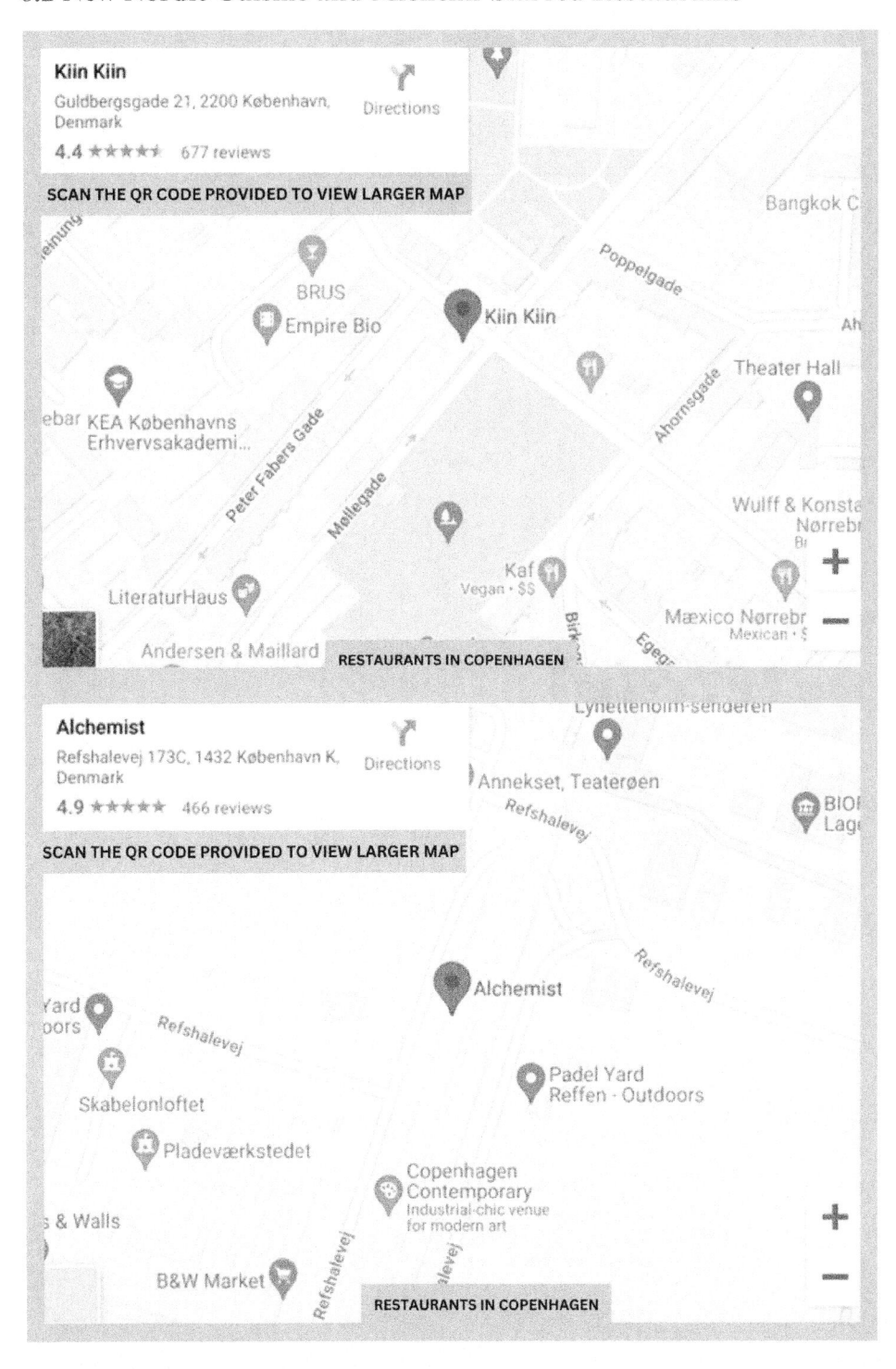

Kiin Kiin
Guldbergsgade 21, 2200 København, Denmark
4.4 ★★★★ 677 reviews

SCAN THE QR CODE PROVIDED TO VIEW LARGER MAP

RESTAURANTS IN COPENHAGEN

Alchemist
Refshalevej 173C, 1432 København K, Denmark
4.9 ★★★★★ 466 reviews

SCAN THE QR CODE PROVIDED TO VIEW LARGER MAP

RESTAURANTS IN COPENHAGEN

Geranium
Per Henrik Lings Allé 4, 8. Sal, 2100
København, Denmark
4.7 ★★★★★ 770 reviews

SCAN THE QR CODE PROVIDED TO VIEW LARGER MAP

RESTAURANTS IN COPENHAGEN

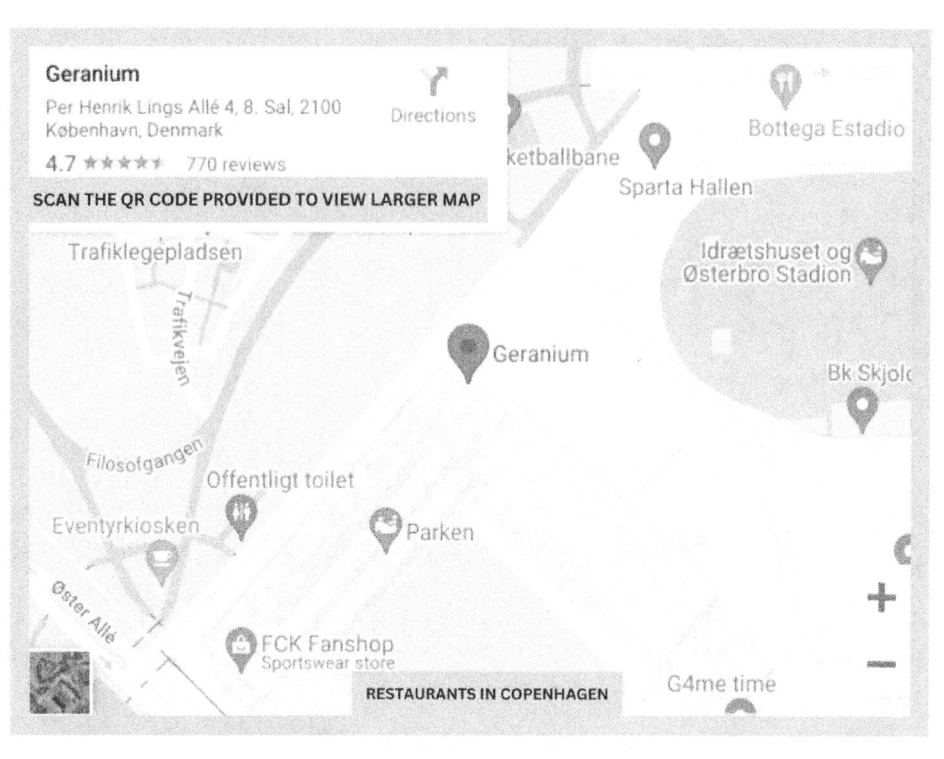

Scan the QR Code with a device to view a comprehensive and larger map of various Restaurants in Copenhagen

In the vibrant culinary landscape of Copenhagen, the New Nordic Cuisine has emerged as a beacon of innovation and creativity, drawing food enthusiasts from around the globe to experience its unique flavors and philosophies. Here are several Michelin-starred restaurants stand out as exemplars of this culinary movement, each offering a distinctive experience

Noma, often hailed as the pioneer of New Nordic Cuisine, remains an undisputed gem in Copenhagen's culinary crown. Situated in the picturesque Christianshavn neighborhood, Noma boasts an ever-evolving menu that celebrates seasonal, locally-sourced ingredients in innovative ways. Diners can expect a culinary journey that transcends traditional boundaries, with dishes that beautifully marry bold flavors and delicate nuances. While the price point at Noma is undeniably high, the experience of dining here is truly unparalleled, making it a must-visit destination for gastronomes seeking an unforgettable culinary adventure.

Geranium, Located in the heart of Copenhagen's Østerbro district, offers a dining experience that is as visually stunning as it is gastronomically exhilarating. Helmed by acclaimed chef Rasmus Kofoed, Geranium holds three Michelin stars and consistently delights diners with its meticulously crafted tasting menus that showcase the chef's profound respect for nature and seasonality. The restaurant's sleek, modern aesthetic provides the perfect backdrop for an evening of culinary indulgence, while its impeccable service ensures that every guest feels pampered and well-cared-for. While Geranium's prices may be on the higher end, the exquisite dining experience it offers is worth every penny for those with a passion for gastronomy.

Relæ, located in the vibrant Nørrebro district, offers a more casual yet no less impressive take on New Nordic Cuisine. Led by chef Christian Puglisi, Relæ has earned a Michelin star for its innovative approach to sustainable dining, with a focus on organic and biodynamic ingredients sourced from local farmers and producers. Diners can expect dishes that are both inventive and unpretentious, showcasing the natural flavors of the ingredients with finesse and creativity. With its relaxed ambiance and affordable pricing, Relæ provides a welcoming introduction to the world of New Nordic Cuisine for both locals and visitors alike.

Kadeau, with its two Michelin stars, offers a culinary journey that celebrates the unique terroir of the Danish islands. Situated in Copenhagen's Christianshavn neighborhood, Kadeau transports diners to the pristine landscapes of Bornholm, where the restaurant's founders hail from. Through a meticulously curated menu that changes with the seasons, Kadeau showcases the bounty of the islands, from wild herbs and foraged delicacies to freshly caught seafood. The restaurant's warm, intimate atmosphere and impeccable service create a dining experience that feels both elegant and deeply personal, making it a favorite among discerning food enthusiasts.

Alchemist, the brainchild of acclaimed chef Rasmus Munk, pushes the boundaries of traditional fine dining with its avant-garde approach to gastronomy. Located in the heart of Copenhagen's former meatpacking district, Alchemist offers a multisensory dining experience that blurs the lines between food, art, and theater. Diners embark on a culinary odyssey through a series of immersive dining rooms, each designed to evoke a different emotion or theme. The menu, which changes regularly, showcases Munk's boundless creativity and culinary prowess, with dishes that challenge conventions and ignite the senses. While dining at Alchemist comes with a hefty price tag, the experience is nothing short of extraordinary, making it a destination worth splurging on for those seeking an unforgettable gastronomic adventure.

Copenhagen's Michelin-starred restaurants represent the pinnacle of New Nordic Cuisine, offering diners an opportunity to experience the rich diversity and creativity of this culinary movement. Whether indulging in the inventive creations of Noma, savoring the seasonal delights of Geranium, or exploring the sustainable ethos of Relæ, visitors to Copenhagen are sure to find themselves captivated by the city's vibrant gastronomic scene.

6.3 Street Food Markets: Torvehallerne and Paper Island

Copenhagen has a vibrant culinary scene that extends to its street food markets. Among the bustling streets and waterfronts, visitors can immerse themselves in the diverse flavors and cultures offered by the city's various street food markets. From traditional Danish delicacies to international cuisines, these markets are a haven for food enthusiasts seeking authentic and delicious experiences.

Torvehallerne: A Culinary Paradise in the Heart of Copenhagen

Torvehallerne stands as a culinary paradise, offering a tantalizing array of gourmet delights. Here, visitors can stroll through two glass-covered market halls brimming with fresh produce, artisanal products, and an impressive selection of street food stalls. The market showcases the best of Danish cuisine, with vendors serving up everything from smørrebrød (open-faced sandwiches) to freshly shucked oysters. For those with a sweet tooth, artisanal chocolates and pastries beckon from every corner.

As for prices, visitors can expect to find a range of options to suit every budget. While some stalls offer affordable bites starting at around 30 DKK ($5 USD), others feature more upscale offerings priced upwards of 100 DKK ($15 USD) or more. It's worth noting that Torvehallerne can get crowded, especially during peak hours, so arriving early or off-peak times can enhance the overall experience.

Paper Island: A Cultural Hub of Street Food Delights

Located on the waterfront near the iconic Nyhavn district, Paper Island (Papirøen) is a cultural hub known for its vibrant street food market. Housed within a former paper warehouse, the market exudes an industrial-chic vibe, with shipping containers transformed into food stalls serving up a diverse array of cuisines from around the world. Prices at Paper Island vary depending on the vendor and the complexity of the dish, but most offerings are reasonably priced, with many options available for under 100 DKK ($15 USD).

Reffen: Where Creativity Meets Sustainability

For those seeking a more eclectic and environmentally conscious dining experience, Reffen offers a unique blend of creativity and sustainability. Situated in the industrial-chic neighborhood of Refshaleøen, this outdoor street food market features a mix of food stalls, art installations, and communal dining areas set against the backdrop of repurposed shipping containers and graffiti-adorned walls.

Værnedamsvej: A Hidden Gem in the Vesterbro District

Tucked away in the trendy Vesterbro district, Værnedamsvej offers a charming escape from the hustle and bustle of the city center. This quaint street is lined with cozy cafes, boutique shops, and specialty food stores, including several vendors selling delicious street food fare. Visitors can indulge in gourmet hot dogs, freshly baked pastries, and artisanal cheeses, all while soaking up the neighborhood's relaxed vibe.

Streat Food: A Mobile Feast on Wheels

Beyond the fixed marketplaces, Copenhagen's street food scene extends to a vibrant array of food trucks and pop-up stalls scattered throughout the city. From iconic hot dog stands to gourmet burger joints, these mobile eateries offer a convenient and delicious way to sample local flavors on the go. Whether you're craving traditional Danish smørrebrød or exotic street food fusion, there's no shortage of options to satisfy your culinary cravings. Prices at streat food vendors vary depending on the location and the type of cuisine, but most offerings are budget-friendly, with many items priced under 100 DKK ($15 USD). Visitors can easily spot food trucks parked in popular areas like Kongens Nytorv or

Nørrebro, where they can grab a quick bite while exploring the city's attractions.

Copenhagen's street food markets offer a tantalizing journey through the city's culinary landscape, showcasing a diverse array of flavors, cultures, and culinary traditions. Whether you're savoring smørrebrød at Torvehallerne, feasting on global cuisines at Paper Island, or exploring the creative offerings at Reffen, each market promises a unique and unforgettable dining experience.

6.4 Coffee Culture and Danish Pastries

Copenhagen lies a vibrant coffee culture that beckons visitors to indulge in the art of slow living and culinary delights. From quaint coffee shops to bustling cafes, the Danish capital offers a diverse array of experiences for coffee enthusiasts and pastry aficionados alike. Embark on a journey through Copenhagen's bustling streets and discover the rich tapestry of flavors, aromas, and traditions that define its coffee culture and Danish pastries.

Kaffe and Kage: A Danish Tradition

Central to Danish culture is the concept of *"kaffe og kage"* (coffee and cake), a cherished tradition that brings people together to enjoy moments of relaxation and indulgence. In Copenhagen, visitors can experience this tradition firsthand at charming cafes like Café Europa or Original Coffee, where freshly brewed coffee is paired with an array of delectable pastries. From flaky croissants to indulgent cinnamon rolls, these cafes offer a delightful selection of treats to accompany your coffee experience. Prices for a cup of coffee typically range from 30 to 50 Danish kroner, while pastries can vary in price depending on the type and size, usually ranging from 20 to 50 Danish kroner each.

Danish Pastries: A Taste of Tradition

No visit to Copenhagen would be complete without sampling the iconic Danish pastries that have captured the hearts of locals and visitors alike. From the buttery layers of a classic Danish pastry to the sweet indulgence of a fruit-filled snegl, these pastries are a true testament to Danish craftsmanship and culinary expertise. For an authentic experience, head to renowned bakeries such as Andersen Bakery or Lagkagehuset, where you can savor a variety of traditional Danish pastries made with the finest ingredients and time-honored techniques. Prices for Danish pastries typically range from 20 to 50 Danish kroner each, depending on the size and ingredients.

Smørrebrød: Coffee's Perfect Companion

In Copenhagen's coffee culture, Smørrebrød serves as the perfect companion to a leisurely cup of coffee. These open-faced sandwiches, adorned with an array of savory toppings, offer a delightful contrast to the rich flavors of coffee and provide a satisfying snack for visitors exploring the city's cafes and bakeries. For a taste of traditional Smørrebrød, visit establishments like Aamanns Deli & Take Away or Schønnemanns Restaurant & Bar, where you can indulge in classic variations such as herring with onions and capers or roast beef with remoulade. Prices for Smørrebrød typically range from 60 to 120 Danish kroner per piece, depending on the toppings and venue.

Hygge: Embracing Danish Coziness

At the heart of Copenhagen's coffee culture and pastry tradition lies the concept of "hygge," a Danish term that embodies coziness, contentment, and a sense of well-being. Whether enjoying a cup of coffee by the waterfront or indulging in a warm pastry on a chilly afternoon, visitors are invited to embrace the simple pleasures of life and immerse themselves in the warmth and hospitality of Danish culture. When exploring Copenhagen's cafes and bakeries, take the time to slow down, savor the moment, and appreciate the beauty of everyday rituals that make Danish coffee culture truly special.

Copenhagen's coffee culture and Danish pastries is a journey of discovery, where each sip of coffee and bite of pastry tells a story of tradition, craftsmanship, and a deep connection to Danish heritage. From the bustling cafes of the city center to the quaint bakeries of the suburbs, visitors are invited to immerse themselves in the rich tapestry of flavors, aromas, and traditions that define Copenhagen's culinary landscape.

6.5 Food Tours and Cooking Classes

Copenhagen, a city brimming with cultural diversity and gastronomic wonders, offers a tantalizing array of food tours and cooking classes for both locals and visitors alike. From traditional Danish delicacies to international fusion cuisine, there's something to suit every palate. Embark on a culinary adventure through the cobblestone streets of Copenhagen and immerse yourself in the rich flavors and culinary traditions of this vibrant city.

Nordic Food Lovers Tour

Step into the heart of Copenhagen's food scene with the Nordic Food Lovers Tour, a guided culinary journey curated to showcase the best of Nordic cuisine. Sold through local tour agencies and online platforms, this immersive experience takes participants on a gastronomic exploration through the city's top food markets, artisanal bakeries, and renowned restaurants. Priced at approximately 800 DKK per person, the tour includes tastings of traditional Nordic dishes such as smørrebrød (open-faced sandwiches), herring, and Danish pastries. Tips for visitors: Come hungry and be prepared to indulge in a feast of flavors. Wear comfortable walking shoes as the tour involves strolling through various neighborhoods and marketplaces.

New Nordic Cooking Class

Delve deeper into the culinary traditions of Scandinavia with a hands-on cooking class focused on New Nordic cuisine. Offered by local cooking schools and culinary academies, this interactive experience provides participants with the opportunity to learn from skilled chefs and master the art of preparing contemporary Nordic dishes. Prices for cooking classes typically range from 600 to 1000 DKK per person, depending on the duration and inclusions. Visitors can expect to whip up dishes like smoked salmon with dill cream, pickled vegetables, and rye bread under the guidance of expert instructors. Relevant tips: Book in advance as classes often fill up quickly, and don't forget to bring a camera to capture your culinary creations.

Copenhagen Street Food Market Tour

For a taste of Copenhagen's vibrant street food scene, embark on a guided tour of the city's bustling food markets and pop-up stalls. Available through local tour operators, this gastronomic adventure introduces participants to a diverse array of international cuisines, from Mexican tacos to Thai noodles. Priced at around 500 DKK per person, the tour includes samplings of street food specialties and insights into the cultural influences shaping Copenhagen's culinary landscape. Tips for visitors: Come with an open mind and a willingness to try new flavors. Be prepared for crowds, especially during peak hours, and bring cash as some vendors may not accept credit cards.

Traditional Danish Cooking Workshop

Immerse yourself in the timeless traditions of Danish cuisine with a hands-on cooking workshop led by local culinary experts. Sold through boutique cooking schools and cultural centers, these intimate sessions offer participants the chance to learn age-old recipes and cooking techniques passed down through generations. Prices typically range from 700 to 1200 DKK per person, inclusive of ingredients and equipment. During the workshop, participants can expect to prepare classic dishes such as frikadeller (Danish meatballs), æbleflæsk (apple and pork stew), and æbleskiver (Danish pancakes). Relevant tips: Check for any dietary restrictions or allergies when booking, and arrive on time to make the most of the experience.

Vegetarian and Vegan Food Tour

Discover the plant-based delights of Copenhagen with a specialized vegetarian and vegan food tour designed to showcase the city's diverse range of meat-free options. Offered by eco-conscious tour operators and food enthusiasts, this guided excursion highlights sustainable dining practices and introduces participants to innovative plant-based dishes. Prices for the tour start at approximately 600 DKK per person, inclusive of tastings and insights into Copenhagen's burgeoning vegetarian scene. Tips for visitors: Notify the tour organizers of any dietary preferences or restrictions in advance, and be prepared to sample a variety of creative vegetarian and vegan dishes from local eateries and cafes.

From traditional Danish fare to contemporary culinary innovations, Copenhagen offers a myriad of food tours and cooking classes for enthusiasts of all tastes and preferences. Whether you're a seasoned foodie or a curious traveler eager to explore the city's gastronomic delights, there's no shortage of delicious experiences awaiting you in the Danish capital.

CHAPTER 7
DAY TRIPS AND EXCURSIONS

7.1 Frederiksborg Castle and Kronborg Castle

Embarking on day trips from Copenhagen unveils a treasure trove of historical landmarks, picturesque landscapes, and immersive experiences that promise to captivate visitors.

Frederiksborg Castle: A Majestic Renaissance Marvel

Situated in the charming town of Hillerød, approximately 40 kilometers northwest of Copenhagen, Frederiksborg Castle stands as a testament to Denmark's rich heritage and royal legacy. As visitors approach the castle, they are greeted by its breathtaking facade, adorned with ornate spires, grand towers, and intricate sculptures. A symbol of Danish cultural pride, Frederiksborg Castle is renowned for its opulent interior, featuring lavishly decorated chambers, stately halls, and a remarkable collection of art and historical artifacts.

To reach Frederiksborg Castle from Copenhagen, travelers can opt for various transportation modes, including train, bus, or car rental. The journey typically takes around 45 minutes by train, offering passengers scenic views of the Danish countryside along the way. Ticket prices for a round-trip train journey range from 100 to 200 DKK, depending on the class and time of travel.

Kronborg Castle: Immersed in Shakespearean Lore
Perched majestically on the northeastern tip of the island of Zealand, Kronborg Castle beckons visitors with its imposing fortress walls and maritime charm. Renowned as the setting for William Shakespeare's timeless tragedy, "Hamlet," Kronborg Castle exudes an aura of mystery and intrigue, inviting guests to delve into its rich history and legendary tales. From the towering ramparts, visitors can gaze out across the Øresund Strait, marveling at panoramic views of the Swedish coastline.

Accessing Kronborg Castle from Copenhagen is convenient and straightforward, with frequent train services connecting the two destinations. The journey takes approximately 40 minutes, offering passengers a scenic ride along the coastline. Round-trip train tickets typically cost between 100 and 150 DKK, making it an affordable option for day trippers.

Roskilde: Where Viking Heritage Meets Modernity

Just a short journey southwest of Copenhagen lies the historic city of Roskilde, a UNESCO World Heritage Site celebrated for its rich Viking heritage and contemporary cultural scene. Home to the iconic Roskilde Cathedral, a masterpiece of Gothic architecture, the city also boasts the Viking Ship Museum, where visitors can marvel at beautifully preserved Viking longships dating back over a thousand years.

Traveling from Copenhagen to Roskilde is convenient, with frequent train services departing from Copenhagen Central Station. The journey takes approximately 25 minutes, offering passengers ample time to soak in the picturesque landscapes of rural Zealand. Round-trip train tickets are priced at around 100 DKK, making it an affordable and accessible day trip option.

Embarking on day trips from Copenhagen unveils a world of discovery and adventure, where centuries-old castles, cultural landmarks, and natural wonders await exploration. With convenient transportation options, affordable ticket prices, and a wealth of experiences to be had, day trippers are sure to be enchanted by the wonders of Northern Zealand.

7.2 Roskilde: Viking Ship Museum and Cathedral

Just a stone's throw away from Copenhagen lies the historic city of Roskilde, a treasure trove of Viking history, medieval architecture, and cultural heritage. For travelers seeking a day trip rich in exploration and immersion, Roskilde offers a plethora of attractions to captivate the imagination and engage the senses.

Transportation and Distance

Embarking on this journey from Copenhagen to Roskilde is seamless, with various transportation options available. The most convenient mode of travel is by train, with regular departures from Copenhagen Central Station to Roskilde Station, covering a distance of approximately 30 kilometers. The train ride offers scenic views of the Danish countryside, enhancing the overall experience of the journey. The cost of a round-trip train ticket typically ranges from 100 to 200 DKK, depending on the type of ticket and time of travel.

Viking Ship Museum

Upon arrival in Roskilde, visitors are greeted by the imposing presence of the Viking Ship Museum, an architectural marvel situated along the picturesque shores of the Roskilde Fjord. Stepping inside the museum is akin to stepping back in time, as it houses a remarkable collection of well-preserved Viking ships, each with its own fascinating story to tell. Visitors can marvel at the craftsmanship of these ancient vessels, explore interactive exhibits, and even participate in hands-on activities such as boat building and sailing simulations. The museum offers guided tours and educational programs, providing insights into the seafaring prowess and cultural legacy of the Vikings.

Roskilde Cathedral

Dominating the city skyline with its towering spires and Gothic architecture, Roskilde Cathedral stands as a testament to Denmark's rich religious heritage and royal history. As the final resting place of numerous Danish monarchs, including Queen Margrethe I and King Christian IV, the cathedral exudes an aura of grandeur and solemnity. Visitors can admire its ornate interiors adorned with intricate frescoes, majestic tombs, and stunning stained glass windows. Guided tours offer a deeper understanding of the cathedral's significance and its role in shaping Danish identity over the centuries.

Roskilde Museum

For those eager to delve deeper into Roskilde's past, a visit to the Roskilde Museum is highly recommended. Housed in a charming 18th-century building, the museum showcases a diverse collection of artifacts, artworks, and archaeological finds spanning the city's history from prehistoric times to the present day. Highlights include exhibits on Roskilde's maritime heritage, medieval craftsmanship, and contemporary culture. Interactive displays and multimedia installations offer engaging insights into the daily lives of past inhabitants, making history come alive for visitors of all ages.

Roskilde Gardens and Parks

After a day of exploration, visitors can unwind amidst the tranquil beauty of Roskilde's gardens and parks, which offer idyllic settings for relaxation and leisure. The Viking Ship Museum's waterfront location provides scenic views of the fjord, ideal for leisurely strolls or picnics overlooking the water. Nearby parks such as Folkeparken and Sct. Jørgensbjerg Park offer lush green spaces, playgrounds, and walking trails, perfect for enjoying the fresh air and natural surroundings.

A day trip from Copenhagen to Roskilde promises an enriching and unforgettable experience, immersing visitors in the fascinating world of Viking history, medieval architecture, and cultural heritage. With its convenient accessibility, diverse attractions, and scenic beauty, Roskilde beckons travelers to embark on a journey of discovery and exploration, leaving indelible memories to cherish for a lifetime.

7.3 Louisiana Museum of Modern Art

Tucked away amidst the tranquil landscapes of northern Zealand lies the Louisiana Museum of Modern Art, a beacon of creativity and cultural enrichment. Renowned for its stunning collection of contemporary art and its seamless integration with nature, the museum offers visitors a unique and immersive experience unlike any other. As guests approach the museum, they are greeted by its striking architecture, characterized by sleek lines and expansive glass windows that blur the boundaries between indoor and outdoor spaces.

Transportation and Accessibility

Located approximately 35 kilometers north of Copenhagen, accessing the Louisiana Museum of Modern Art is both convenient and straightforward. Travelers can embark on a scenic train journey from Copenhagen Central Station, which takes approximately 40 minutes and offers breathtaking views of the Danish coastline along the way.

Round-trip train tickets are priced at around 100-150 DKK, making it an affordable option for day trippers. Alternatively, visitors can opt for a bus or car rental, with ample parking available near the museum.

Art Amidst Nature

Upon arrival, visitors are greeted by the museum's sprawling grounds, which are meticulously landscaped to complement the surrounding natural beauty. Sculpture gardens dotted with contemporary artworks provide a serene setting for contemplation and reflection, while winding pathways lead guests on a journey of discovery through lush greenery and panoramic sea views. Inside the museum, a world of artistic innovation awaits, with galleries showcasing works by renowned artists such as Picasso, Warhol, and Giacometti.

Interactive Exhibitions and Cultural Events

In addition to its permanent collection, the Louisiana Museum of Modern Art regularly hosts temporary exhibitions and cultural events that showcase the diversity of contemporary art and culture. From multimedia installations to interactive workshops and artist talks, there is always something new and exciting to explore at the museum. Visitors are encouraged to check the museum's website for upcoming events and exhibitions to make the most of their visit.

Culinary Delights and Souvenir Shopping

After a day of art appreciation, visitors can indulge in culinary delights at the museum's on-site café, which offers a selection of Danish delicacies and international cuisine. With its panoramic views of the Øresund Strait, the café provides the perfect spot to relax and unwind amidst the picturesque surroundings. For those looking to take home a piece of the Louisiana Museum of Modern Art, the museum shop offers a curated selection of art books, prints, and souvenirs inspired by the museum's collection.

A day trip to the Louisiana Museum of Modern Art offers visitors a unique opportunity to immerse themselves in the beauty of contemporary art amidst the serenity of nature. With convenient transportation options, affordable ticket prices, and a wealth of cultural experiences to be had, the museum is a must-see destination for art enthusiasts and nature lovers alike.

7.4 Malmö, Sweden: Öresund Bridge and Old Town

One of the most iconic landmarks connecting Copenhagen to Malmö is the Öresund Bridge, a breathtaking feat of engineering that spans the Øresund Strait. As visitors embark on their journey across this architectural marvel, they are treated to panoramic views of the sparkling waters below and the distant shores of Sweden on the horizon. The bridge, which stretches over 8 kilometers in length, serves as a symbolic link between Denmark and Sweden, embodying the spirit of cross-border cooperation and connectivity.

Transportation and Accessibility

Traveling from Copenhagen to Malmö is a seamless experience, thanks to the efficient transportation options available. For those looking to make the journey by train, frequent services depart from Copenhagen

Central Station, offering a scenic ride across the Öresund Bridge and into the heart of Malmö. The journey typically takes around 35 minutes, with round-trip tickets priced at approximately 200-250 DKK. Alternatively, travelers can opt for a bus or car rental, with convenient parking facilities available near the city center.

Old Town: A Quaint Journey Through History

Upon arrival in Malmö, visitors are greeted by the charming cobblestone streets and medieval architecture of the Old Town, known locally as Gamla Staden. Steeped in history and tradition, this picturesque neighborhood invites guests to wander its narrow alleyways, past colorful merchant houses and inviting cafes. Highlights include Stortorget, the main square lined with centuries-old buildings, and Lilla Torg, a bustling plaza surrounded by quaint shops and lively restaurants.

Malmö Castle: A Glimpse into the Past

Perched majestically on the banks of the Malmö River, Malmö Castle stands as a symbol of the city's rich history and cultural heritage. Dating back to the 16th century, the castle offers visitors a glimpse into Sweden's royal past, with its imposing fortress walls, regal interiors, and fascinating museum exhibits. From the castle grounds, guests can enjoy panoramic views of the surrounding cityscape and the verdant gardens that stretch out along the riverbank.

Turning Torso: A Modern Architectural Marvel

For a taste of contemporary design and innovation, visitors to Malmö should not miss the iconic Turning Torso skyscraper. Dominating the city skyline with its sleek, twisting form, this architectural marvel stands as the tallest building in Scandinavia and a symbol of Malmö's modernity and progress. Guests can admire the tower from afar or venture inside for a guided tour, where they can learn about the building's unique construction and groundbreaking design.

Malmö's Culinary Scene: A Gastronomic Adventure
No visit to Malmö would be complete without indulging in its vibrant culinary scene, which offers a diverse array of flavors and cuisines to suit every palate. From traditional Swedish delicacies to international fusion cuisine, the city's restaurants and eateries are sure to tantalize the taste buds of even the most discerning food lovers. Whether savoring fresh seafood by the waterfront or sampling street food delights in the bustling markets, visitors are in for a gastronomic adventure like no other.

A day trip to Malmö from Copenhagen promises an unforgettable journey of exploration and discovery, where ancient history and modern innovation converge in a vibrant tapestry of culture and charm. With convenient transportation options, affordable ticket prices, and a wealth of attractions to explore, visitors are sure to be enchanted by the wonders of this iconic Swedish city.

7.5 Hillerød: Frederiksborg Castle and Baroque Gardens
Just a short journey from the bustling streets of Copenhagen lies the quaint town of Hillerød, a hidden gem brimming with history, culture, and natural beauty. A day trip to Hillerød offers travelers the opportunity to immerse themselves in the opulence of Danish royalty, stroll through

enchanting gardens, and explore charming cobblestone streets lined with historic buildings.

Transportation and Distance

Embarking on this adventure from Copenhagen to Hillerød is both convenient and affordable, with various transportation options available to suit every traveler's preference. The most popular mode of travel is by train, with frequent departures from Copenhagen Central Station to Hillerød Station, covering a distance of approximately 40 kilometers. The train journey offers scenic views of the Danish countryside, providing a relaxing and enjoyable travel experience. The cost of a round-trip train ticket typically ranges from 100 to 200 DKK, depending on factors such as ticket type and time of travel.

Frederiksborg Castle

Upon arrival in Hillerød, visitors are greeted by the majestic silhouette of Frederiksborg Castle, a masterpiece of Renaissance architecture and the crown jewel of Danish castles. Situated on the shores of Lake Slotsø, the castle boasts a rich history dating back to the 17th century, when it served as the royal residence of King Christian IV. Today, it stands as a museum showcasing a remarkable collection of art, furniture, and decorative objects from Denmark's past. Visitors can explore the lavish interiors of the castle, including the Great Hall, Chapel, and Audience Chamber, adorned with intricate woodcarvings, tapestries, and ceiling paintings. Guided tours provide fascinating insights into the lives of Danish royalty and the castle's significance as a cultural heritage site.

Baroque Gardens

Adjacent to Frederiksborg Castle lies the picturesque Baroque Gardens, a tranquil oasis of manicured lawns, vibrant flower beds, and ornamental fountains. Designed in the 17th century by renowned landscape architect Johan Cornelius Krieger, the gardens offer a delightful blend of formal symmetry and natural beauty. Visitors can meander along winding pathways, marvel at sculpted hedges and topiaries, and relax amidst the serene ambiance of this historic green space. The gardens provide the perfect backdrop for leisurely strolls, romantic picnics, and memorable photo opportunities overlooking the castle and lake.

Hillerød Old Town

For those eager to explore Hillerød's charming town center, a visit to the Old Town is a must. Lined with colorful half-timbered houses, cobblestone streets, and quaint cafes, the Old Town exudes a timeless charm reminiscent of a bygone era. Visitors can wander through narrow alleyways, browse boutique shops selling local crafts and souvenirs, and savor traditional Danish cuisine at cozy restaurants and eateries. Highlights include the historic Town Hall Square, St. Nicolai Church, and the lively weekly market offering fresh produce and artisanal goods.

Lake Slotsø and Surrounding Nature

Nature enthusiasts will delight in the scenic beauty surrounding Lake Slotsø, which provides ample opportunities for outdoor recreation and exploration. Visitors can rent rowboats or pedal boats to glide across the tranquil waters of the lake, taking in panoramic views of Frederiksborg Castle and its reflection shimmering in the water. The surrounding parkland offers idyllic picnic spots, walking trails, and wildlife observation areas, allowing visitors to connect with nature and unwind amidst the serene landscape.

A day trip from Copenhagen to Hillerød promises a memorable journey through Danish royalty and baroque splendor, offering a rich tapestry of history, culture, and natural beauty to explore and enjoy. With its convenient accessibility, diverse attractions, and enchanting ambiance, Hillerød beckons travelers to embark on a captivating adventure, leaving them with cherished memories and a deeper appreciation for Denmark's rich heritage.

CHAPTER 8
ENTERTAINMENT AND NIGHTLIFE

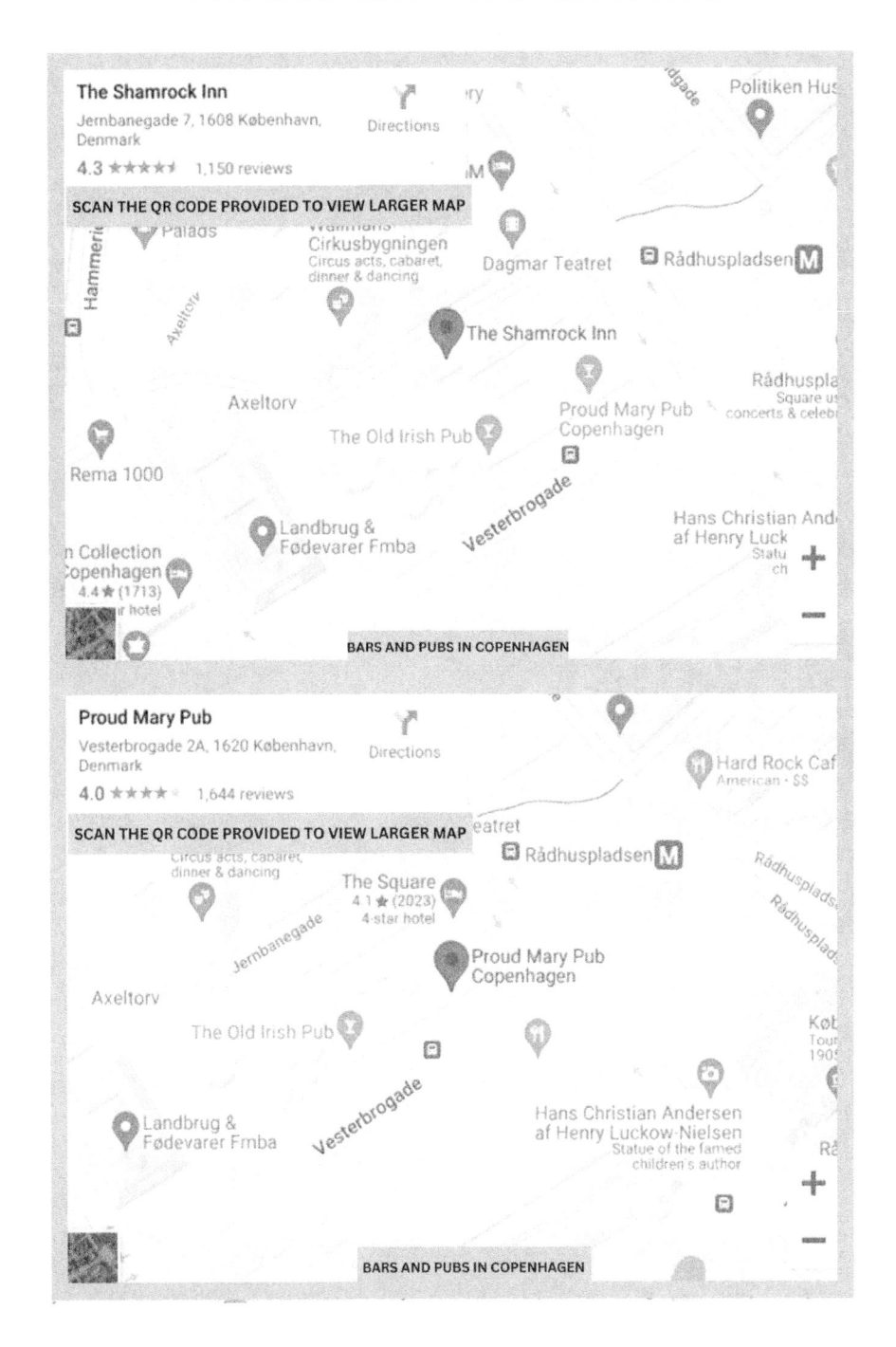

The Shamrock Inn
Jernbanegade 7, 1608 København, Denmark
4.3 ★★★★★ 1,150 reviews

SCAN THE QR CODE PROVIDED TO VIEW LARGER MAP

BARS AND PUBS IN COPENHAGEN

Proud Mary Pub
Vesterbrogade 2A, 1620 København, Denmark
4.0 ★★★★ 1,644 reviews

SCAN THE QR CODE PROVIDED TO VIEW LARGER MAP

BARS AND PUBS IN COPENHAGEN

Freddys Bar
Gasværksvej 28, 1656 København, Denmark
4.3 ★★★★☆ 560 reviews

SCAN THE QR CODE PROVIDED TO VIEW LARGER MAP

BARS AND PUBS IN COPENHAGEN

Scan the QR Code with a device to view a comprehensive and larger map of various Bars and Pubs in Copenhagen

8.1 Cafés and Bars in Nørrebro and Vesterbro

As the sun sets, the streets come alive with the promise of unforgettable experiences, particularly in the eclectic neighborhoods of Nørrebro and Vesterbro, among others. Embark on a journey through Copenhagen's vibrant nightlife, where each café and bar is a portal to a world of excitement and discovery.

Nørrebro: A Bohemian Wonderland

In the bustling district of Nørrebro, adventure awaits around every corner. Dive into the soulful ambiance of cozy cafés and lively bars, where the air is thick with laughter and the scent of freshly brewed coffee. Wander through the cobblestone streets until you stumble upon Café Retro, a beloved local haunt known for its laid-back atmosphere and affordable prices. Sip on a steaming cup of organic coffee as you soak in the eclectic décor, adorned with vintage furniture and colorful artwork. With its cozy nooks and welcoming vibe, Café Retro is the perfect spot to unwind after a day of exploration.

Vesterbro: Where Creativity Flourishes

Venture south to the vibrant district of Vesterbro, where creativity flourishes amidst the urban landscape. Here, tucked away in a charming corner, lies Ruby Cocktail Bar, a hidden gem awaiting discovery. Step through the doors and be transported to a world of sophistication and elegance, where expert mixologists craft exquisite cocktails with precision and flair. Indulge in a signature concoction as you bask in the warm glow of candlelight, surrounded by velvet drapes and plush seating.

With its intimate ambiance and impeccable service, Ruby Cocktail Bar offers a taste of luxury that is sure to leave a lasting impression.

Indre By: Uncovering Hidden Gems

In the historic district of Indre By, history and modernity collide to create a tapestry of experiences waiting to be uncovered. Venture off the beaten path and discover Lidkoeb, a rustic hideaway nestled within a converted townhouse. Ascend the staircase to find yourself in a cozy loft space adorned with exposed brick walls and flickering candlelight. Take a seat at the bar and embark on a journey through the world of whiskey, with an extensive selection of rare and unique spirits to choose from. With its intimate ambiance and expertly crafted cocktails, Lidkoeb offers a sanctuary from the hustle and bustle of the city, where time seems to stand still.

In Copenhagen, the night is alive with possibility, beckoning you to explore its myriad wonders. From cozy cafés to chic cocktail bars, each establishment offers a unique glimpse into the rich tapestry of Danish culture and hospitality. So, grab a friend, raise a glass, and let the magic of Copenhagen's nightlife sweep you away on an unforgettable adventure.

8.2 Live Music Venues and Jazz Clubs

Copenhagen isn't just renowned for its stunning architecture and bicycle-friendly streets; it's also a hub for nightlife and entertainment. Dive into the city's after-dark scene, and you'll discover a world of live music venues and jazz clubs that pulsate with energy and creativity. Let's embark on a journey through diverse establishments that showcase Copenhagen's rich musical tapestry.

Melodic Marvels at Jazzhus Montmartre

Inthe heart of the historic Latin Quarter, Jazzhus Montmartre stands as a beacon of Copenhagen's jazz legacy. Stepping into this intimate venue feels like entering a time capsule to the golden era of jazz. The ambiance is electric, with low lighting casting a warm glow over the vintage decor. Savvy locals and in-the-know travelers gather here to revel in the soulful tunes performed by both established artists and up-and-coming talents. From sultry saxophones to lively improvisations, each night at Jazzhus Montmartre promises a melodic journey through the heart of jazz.

Enchanting Evenings at La Fontaine

Tucked away in a charming alley off Strøget, Copenhagen's bustling pedestrian street, La Fontaine exudes an air of enchantment that captivates visitors from the moment they step inside. This cozy jazz club boasts an eclectic lineup of musicians, spanning genres from traditional jazz to experimental fusion. The intimate setting fosters a sense of camaraderie among patrons, who gather around candlelit tables to savor expertly crafted cocktails and immerse themselves in the music. With its inviting atmosphere and top-notch performances, La Fontaine offers an unforgettable evening of sonic exploration.

Groove to the Beat at Mojo Blues Bar

For aficionados of the blues, Mojo Blues Bar is a pilgrimage site not to be missed. Located in the heart of Copenhagen's vibrant Nørrebro district, this iconic venue pulsates with raw energy and gritty authenticity. Stepping through the door, visitors are greeted by the soulful strains of blues music that permeate the dimly lit space. From electrifying guitar solos to impassioned vocals, the performances at Mojo Blues Bar are nothing short of electrifying. Whether you're a seasoned blues enthusiast or a newcomer to the genre, you'll find yourself swept away by the irresistible groove that permeates this legendary establishment.

Eclectic Vibes at VEGA

Venture to the trendy Vesterbro district, and you'll discover VEGA, a multifaceted entertainment complex that promises an eclectic mix of live music, club nights, and cultural events. Housed within a converted slaughterhouse, VEGA boasts a rich history dating back to the early 20th century. Today, it stands as a beacon of Copenhagen's thriving music scene, hosting an array of international acts alongside local talent. Whether you're in the mood for indie rock, electronic beats, or avant-garde pop, VEGA has something to offer every musical palate. With its dynamic lineup and cutting-edge sound systems, VEGA guarantees an unforgettable night of revelry and discovery.

Underground Vibes at Drone

For those who prefer their nightlife with a dose of underground edge, Drone offers an immersive experience unlike any other. Tucked away beneath the bustling streets of Copenhagen's city center, this subterranean venue pulses with an electrifying energy that draws in a diverse crowd of music lovers and free spirits. The lineup at Drone spans an eclectic range of genres, from experimental electronic to underground hip-hop, ensuring that every visit is a journey into the unknown. With its intimate setting and unapologetically eclectic programming, Drone invites visitors to explore the fringes of Copenhagen's musical landscape and discover hidden gems waiting to be unearthed.

Copenhagen's nightlife scene is a vibrant tapestry woven from a diverse array of musical influences and cultural traditions. Whether you're a jazz aficionado, a blues enthusiast, or simply a lover of live music, the Danish capital offers an abundance of venues where you can immerse yourself in the city's rich musical heritage.

8.3 Beer Bars and Craft Breweries

Amidst the colorful facades of Copenhagen lies a treasure trove of beer bars and craft breweries, each offering a unique glimpse into the city's vibrant nightlife and entertainment scene. As the sun sets and the city comes alive with the buzz of excitement, exploring these hidden gems becomes an adventure in itself, promising unforgettable experiences for beer enthusiasts and curious travelers alike.

Immersing Yourself in Local Flavor at Mikkeller & Friends

One cannot embark on a journey through Copenhagen's beer culture without paying homage to Mikkeller & Friends. Located in the hip neighborhood of Nørrebro, this renowned establishment boasts an extensive selection of craft beers from both local breweries and international favorites. Step inside and be greeted by the warm ambiance of exposed brick walls and cozy seating, inviting you to linger and savor each sip. Prices here may lean towards the higher end, but the quality and diversity of the beer offerings make it a worthwhile indulgence. Don't miss out on their rotating tap list, ensuring that every visit promises a new and exciting discovery.

Uncovering Hidden Gems at Fermentoren

Tucked away in the bustling streets of Vesterbro lies Fermentoren, a hidden gem beloved by locals and seasoned travelers alike. What sets Fermentoren apart is its commitment to showcasing lesser-known breweries and experimental brews, offering patrons a chance to expand their palate and discover new favorites. The intimate atmosphere and knowledgeable staff create the perfect setting for engaging conversations and shared experiences. While prices may vary depending on the brew, rest assured that each pint is crafted with passion and precision, making every sip a delightful revelation.

Indulging in Tradition at Ølbutikken

For a taste of Copenhagen's rich brewing heritage, look no further than Ølbutikken. Located in the heart of the city center, this cozy beer bar specializes in rare and vintage bottles, providing enthusiasts with a glimpse into the past while celebrating the artistry of brewing. Step through the door and be transported to a world where time seems to stand still, as shelves adorned with meticulously curated selections beckon you to explore. Prices here may reflect the exclusivity of the offerings, but the opportunity to savor a piece of history is truly priceless.

Embracing Creativity at Warpigs Brewpub

Venture across the bridge to the vibrant district of Kødbyen and discover Warpigs Brewpub, a haven for beer lovers and barbecue enthusiasts alike. Housed in a former meatpacking plant, this sprawling brewery and smokehouse exude an industrial charm that sets the stage for an unforgettable experience. Sample their bold and flavorful brews, brewed onsite in collaboration with renowned American brewery Three Floyds, while feasting on mouthwatering barbecue fare. With prices that cater to every budget, Warpigs Brewpub invites you to indulge in a symphony of flavors and textures that will leave you craving more.

Exploring the Uncharted at BRUS

In the heart of Nørrebro, BRUS stands as a testament to Copenhagen's spirit of innovation and experimentation. This multifaceted establishment houses a brewery, bar, and restaurant under one roof, offering visitors a glimpse into the creative process behind their artisanal brews. Step inside and be greeted by sleek, modern interiors that seamlessly blend Scandinavian minimalism with industrial chic. Prices here are reasonable, allowing patrons to sample an array of brews without breaking the bank. Whether you're sipping on a crisp lager or indulging in a decadent sour ale, BRUS invites you to expand your horizons and embrace the unexpected.

In Copenhagen, the night holds endless possibilities for those willing to venture off the beaten path and explore the city's thriving beer culture. From quaint neighborhood bars to innovative brewpubs, each establishment offers a unique glimpse into the rich tapestry of flavors and experiences that define this vibrant city. adventure.

8.4 Nightclubs and Dance Halls

As dusk descends upon the enchanting city of Copenhagen, a new world awakens under the cover of darkness. From the pulsating beats of electronic music to the rhythmic sway of dancers lost in the moment, the nightlife of Copenhagen beckons with promises of exhilaration and liberation. Let's delve into the vibrant tapestry of Copenhagen's nightclubs and dance halls, each offering a unique blend of atmosphere, music, and energy that captivates the soul.

Vega: Where Music Meets Majesty

Vega stands as a beacon of musical diversity and cultural significance. Housed within a historic building dating back to 1956, this iconic venue has played host to some of the world's most renowned artists and performers. Step inside and be greeted by soaring ceilings adorned with intricate chandeliers, creating an ambiance of grandeur and elegance. From indie rock to electronic beats, Vega offers a diverse lineup of concerts and club nights that cater to every musical taste. Immerse yourself in the electrifying energy of the dance floor or simply bask in the beauty of the majestic surroundings.

Culture Box: An Underground Oasis

Hidden away in the vibrant district of Indre By, Culture Box beckons with promises of underground excitement and unbridled creativity. Descend into the depths of this intimate venue and discover a world where the boundaries of electronic music are pushed to their limits. With its state-of-the-art sound system and immersive lighting design, Culture Box offers an unparalleled sensory experience that transcends the ordinary.

KB18: Where Industrial Charm Meets Electronic Ecstasy

Located in the industrial district of Sydhavnen, KB18 exudes an aura of gritty charm and raw energy that sets it apart from the typical nightclub experience. Housed within a converted warehouse, this underground venue serves as a sanctuary for electronic music aficionados seeking refuge from the mainstream. Step inside and be enveloped by the hypnotic sounds of techno and minimal house, reverberating off exposed brick walls and steel beams. With its no-frills approach and dedication to fostering a sense of community, KB18 offers a refreshing alternative to the glitz and glamour of traditional nightclubs. Whether you're a seasoned raver or a curious newcomer, KB18 invites you to embrace the true essence of Copenhagen's underground nightlife.

Rust: A Melting Pot of Culture and Creativity

Perched on the edge of the bustling district of Nørrebro, Rust stands as a testament to Copenhagen's vibrant multicultural landscape. From live music performances to themed club nights, this eclectic venue offers a dynamic array of entertainment options that cater to every taste and inclination. Step inside and be greeted by a colorful collage of artwork and decor, reflecting the diverse influences that shape Copenhagen's cultural identity. Whether you're sipping cocktails in the cozy lounge area or dancing the night away to global beats on the dance floor, Rust provides a welcoming space where creativity knows no bounds. With its commitment to showcasing emerging artists and fostering a sense of inclusivity, Rust embodies the spirit of Copenhagen's cosmopolitan nightlife scene.

Jolene: Where Eclecticism Reigns Supreme

Tucked away in the vibrant district of Nørrebro, Jolene stands as a beacon of eclecticism and artistic expression. Housed within a former car repair shop, this unconventional venue exudes an aura of industrial charm and creative energy that sets it apart from the rest. Step inside and be transported to a world where boundaries blur and imagination runs wild. From live music performances to themed club nights, Jolene offers a diverse array of entertainment options that cater to every mood and inclination. Whether you're sipping craft cocktails at the bar or getting lost in the music on the dance floor, Jolene invites you to embrace the unexpected and celebrate the vibrant tapestry of Copenhagen's nightlife.

In Copenhagen, the night is not merely a time to sleep, but a canvas upon which the city's vibrant spirit comes alive. From historic landmarks to hidden gems, each nightclub and dance hall offers a unique glimpse into the rich tapestry of Danish culture and creativity.

TRAVEL JOURNAL

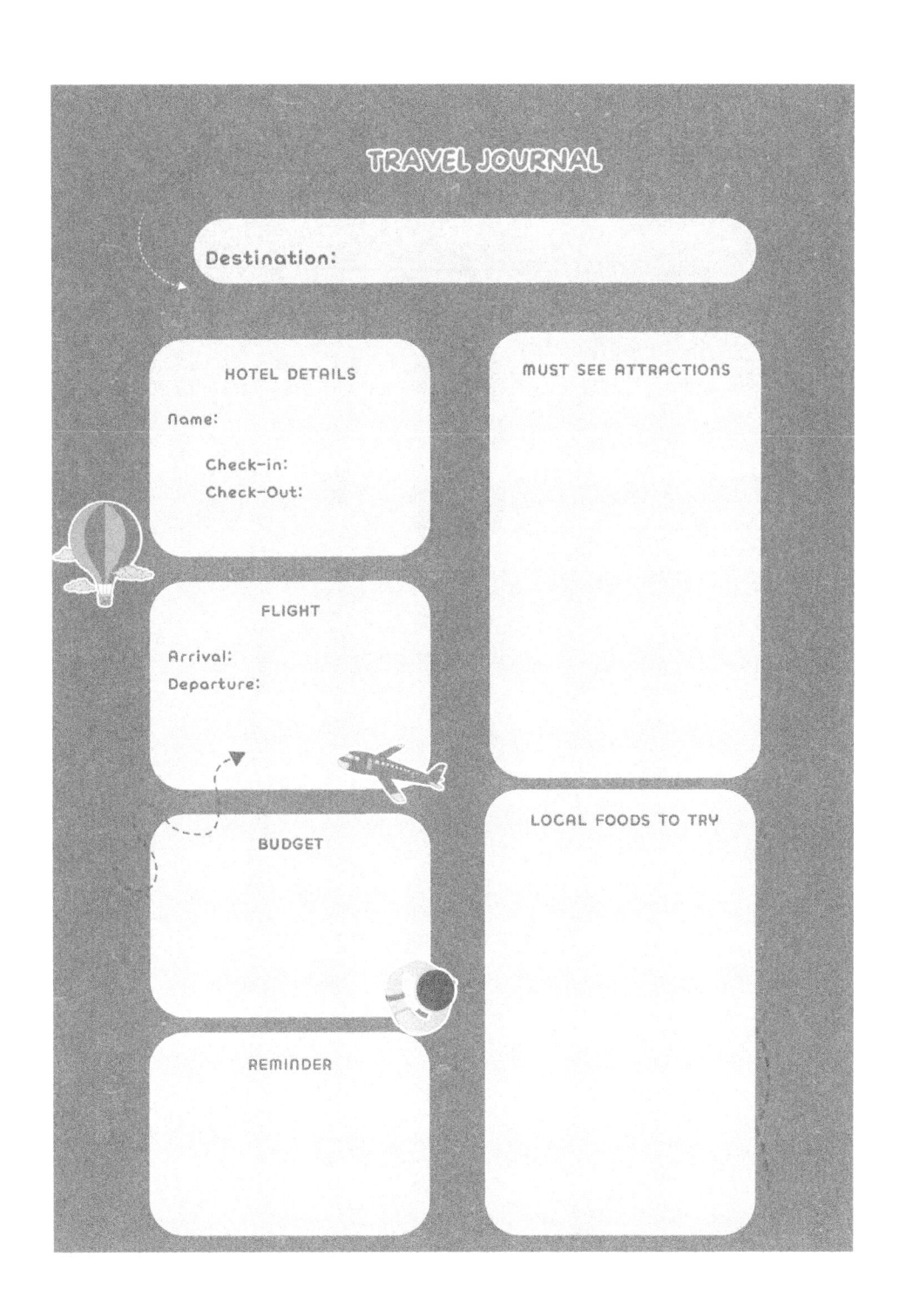

Destination:

HOTEL DETAILS

Name:

Check-in:
Check-Out:

FLIGHT

Arrival:
Departure:

BUDGET

REMINDER

MUST SEE ATTRACTIONS

LOCAL FOODS TO TRY

Packing List

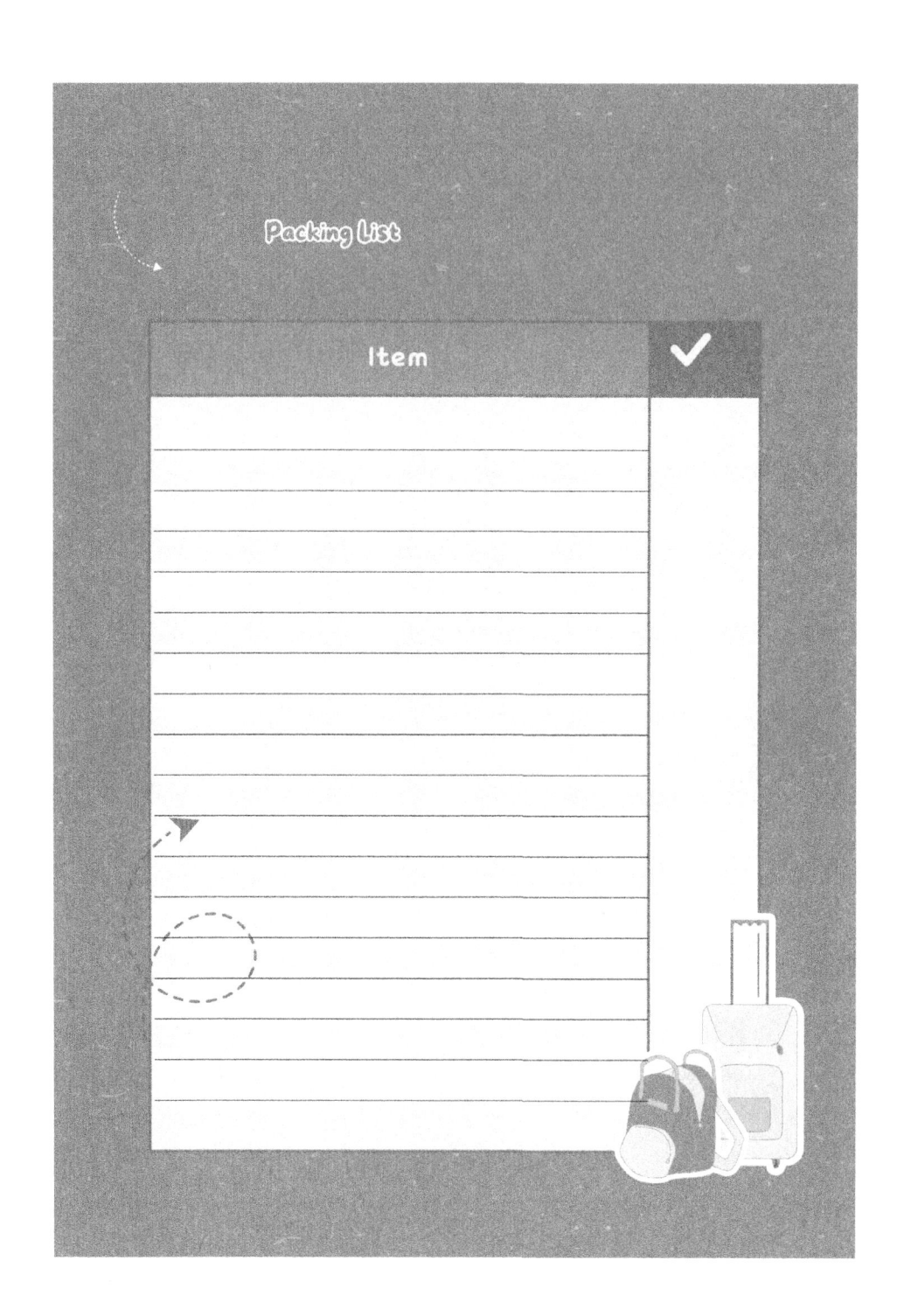

Item	✓

Day 1

Day 2

Day 3

Day 4

Day 5

Day 6

Day 7

MY TRAVEL EXPERIENCE

Printed in Great Britain
by Amazon